China's First Hundred

DATE DUE			

China's First Hundred

Educational Mission Students in the United States

1872-1881

Thomas E. LaFargue

Introduction by Thomas L. Kennedy

Washington State University Press
Pullman, Washington
1987

Printed and bound in the United States of America

Washington State University Press
Pullman, Washington

Library of Congress Cataloging-in-Publication Data

La Fargue, Thomas E. (Thomas Edward), 1900—
    China's first hundred.

    Reprint. Originally published: Pullman: State College of
Washington, 1942.
    Includes index.
    1. Chinese—United States—History—19th century. 2. Chinese—
Education—United States—History—19th century. 3 United States—
Relations—China. 4. China—Relations—United States. 5. China—
Economic conditions—1644-1912. 6. China—Biography. I. Title.
E184.C5L3 1987   973'.04951   87-10404
ISBN 0-87422-035-1 (alk. paper)

This book is printed on pH neutral, acid-free paper.

All Chinese names and terms have been transliterated from Chinese
characters to English using the Wade-Giles method. This was the
method in use when the book was first printed in 1942.

To all that great band of
"returned students"
who have tried to
bridge the gap
between China
and the western world.

CONTENTS

CHINA'S *First* HUNDRED

Thomas E·La Fargue

WESTERN WORLD

PRESS *of the* STATE COLLEGE *of* WASHINGTON *at* PULLMAN

Original dust jacket of *China's First Hundred*.

FOREWORD

Chinese-American friendship; normalization of U.S.-Chinese diplomatic relations; Sino-American cultural, educational and scientific exchange; these phrases are commonplace in the contemporary lexicon of American foreign policy. It is easy to forget, however, that less than two decades ago, China and the United States confronted each other in bitter and uncompromising hostility. But it had not always been that way. From 1941 to 1945, the United States fought Japan in World War II principally to insure the freedom and independence of China. A scant five years later the United States found itself fighting another war in Korea. This time China was the enemy in a struggle that was begun partly to protect the regional security interests of Japan. The history of Chinese-American relations over the last 150 years has been a tangled web, baffling even to scholars and diplomats. To the casual American observer, China's shifts in international policies are truly bewildering.

Occasionally, however, in the literature of Chinese-American relations, there have appeared studies that have made sense of important episodes or trends in the unfolding of this epic encounter, works that have served over the years to interpret China's intentions to Americans, works that have genuinely aided intercultural understanding. *China's First Hundred,* Thomas LaFargue's study of China's first educational mission to the United States is such a work. LaFargue, a faculty member in the Department of History of the State College of Washington, published this study, through the Press of the State College of Washington, at the outset of World War II. Modern sinological research was still in its infancy in the United States and the real issues in Chinese-American relations were obscured by the artificial aura of friendship surrounding the wartime alliance. Still with uncanny prescience, LaFargue distilled from the experience of Chinese students in the United States during the 1870s, some of the principal issues that have persisted in Chinese-American educational exchange in ensuing decades, issues which even today are at the heart of Chinese-American educational relations: the transfer of technology, cultural chauvinism, language acquisition, cultural assimilation and the interrelationships of vastly different educational hierarchies *inter alia.*

In the forty-five years that have elapsed since this slender volume made its appearance in 1942, the story of "China's First Hundred"—the monumental effort of the ailing Qing Dynasty to bring American education to bear on China's problems in adapting to a changing international environment—has continued. Fresh insights and understanding of this ill-starred episode have evolved as historians of the post-war era have uncovered new source materials and brought the research methodology of modern sinology to bear. Furthermore, the study of China's efforts to learn from abroad has broadened to include other educational missions. "China's First Hundred" are now finding their rightful place in a more comprehensive listing of educational missions dispatched overseas. Even more enlightening is the scholarship which places overseas education in the context of China's modernization schemes of the late nineteenth and early twentieth century. Finally, it is with great interest that students of China's modernization greet the recent studies which compare the current Four Modernizations Campaign with China's late nineteenth century modernization. Overseas study, an integral part of both movements, is a key to understanding China's failures of the past and its hopes for the future.

Although this is not the place to review the considerable literature on China's overseas education that has appeared since 1942, Professor LaFargue would be gratified to know that the study which he helped initiate has flourished in many languages. A wealth of new documentation and archival materials has been made available in published collections. Included are official correspondence and memorials to the throne on topics related to overseas education as well as private papers of officials who advocated overseas study and students who participated in the missions. These have provided the basis for important reevaluations of *China's First Hundred* in landmark studies such as William Hung's *Huang Tsung-hsien's poem: The Closure of the Educational Mission in America* (*Harvard Journal of Asiatic Studies*, 18, 1955). Knight Biggerstaff's *The Earliest Modern Government Schools in China* (Ithaca, 1961) reexamines overseas study in the context of a broader investigation of China's educational modernization. More comprehensive in approach are Qu Liho's monograph on overseas study in the late Qing period *Qingmo liuxue jiaoyu*, (Taiwan, an-Min, 1973) and the work of Dong Shouyi on the movement for study abroad during the Qing Dynasty, *Qingdai liuxue yundongshi* (Liaoning People's Press, 1985).

These are only a few of the noteworthy studies that have followed from Professor LaFargue's work. Important research continues. Scholars come and go from the LaFargue collection in the Manuscripts, Archives and Special Collections Division of Washington State University Libraries. Among these is Professor Edwin Pak-wah Leung whose research on "China's First Hundred" should provide a late twentieth century interpretation of the mission as timely and significant as LaFargue's benchmark study at midcentury.

And LaFargue would no doubt have been pleased to read the conclusions of another study of Chinese-Western educational relations conducted in the Department of History of Washington State University some forty years after the publication of *China's First Hundred*. Steven Leibo's doctoral dissertation published as *Transfering Technology to China, Prosper Giquel and the Self-Strengthening Movement* (Berkeley, 1985) concludes with a comparative analysis of China's nineteenth-century modernization and the current Four Modernizations Campaign. Leibo asks the important question: why, when overseas education in America failed to realize its goals, did the mission to Europe prove more successful? He points out some of the remarkable similarities in the situations confronting nineteenth- and twentieth-century modernizers. And he underscores the contemporary problem of a traditional economy and society absorbing the learning and skills brought back by returned students. Leibo's study calls his readers and students to continue the investigation of the root problems complicating the education of Chinese youth in the United States, an investigation which LaFargue initiated in the same academic setting nearly a half century before. With the reissue of this small classic by Washington State University Press, it is my hope that study of problems that beset China's current educational ventures in this country will be stimulated and that new solutions will provide educational benefit to both nations.

Thomas L. Kennedy

Pullman, Washington, 1987

INTRODUCTION

When the smoke of the present world conflict has rolled away and once again events can be viewed in their proper perspective, surely it will become evident that the emergence of China as a strong and independent state is one of the most important phenomena of modern times. The remarkable renaissance which has taken place in China since the last World War goes back to those first few Chinese who had the temerity and courage to break away from the traditions and habits of centuries in order to embark upon the study of western learning. It is from these first pioneers in an alien culture that there have spread and grown the forces which have brought about the China of today. Above all, we must follow the career and influence of Yung Wing, the pioneer of pioneers. Born in 1828 of a peasant family in a little village in South China and never attaining to more than a precarious hold on the lower rungs of the ladder of official preferment, he nevertheless was a true moulder of his people. He was the first Chinese to break through the mental confines of the Middle Kingdom and to view and evaluate the Western World from a Western viewpoint. He was the first Chinese to receive a wholly Occidental education, and from him sprang the revolutionary plan of sending a constant stream of young Chinese lads to the United States to be trained in the technical arts of applied science. The history and results of this effort to provide China with her first engineers, shipbuilders, mining operators, and railroad builders is the theme of this story.

It was not until 1872, after many weary years of effort and disappointments, that Yung Wing saw his scheme for an Educational Mission to the United States actually put into operation. In that year there landed in San Francisco the first group of young Chinese boys sent by the Chinese Government to be educated in the schools and colleges of America. Three other contingents followed until by 1874 there were one hundred and twenty such students living and studying in the schools of a score of small towns scattered throughout the Connecticut Valley. For ten years these boys were busy assimilating their new environment and accumulating the technical knowledge of the various branches of engineering. The original plan proposed that they stay in the United States for fifteen years, then, after a two-year travel period in which they would gain practical experience in what they had learned, they were to return to China to build ships, construct railroads and telegraph lines, and open mines for the Chinese Government. In 1881, however, a swing of political fortunes displaced the sponsors of the Educational Mission and placed in power a group of conservatives who bitterly opposed sending Chinese youths abroad to study the learning of the "western barbarians". The boys were recalled and the Mission was abolished.

The students of the Mission, now young men in their late teens or early twenties, were compelled to return to China only half-prepared to carry out the task for which they had been sent abroad. The order of recall found most of them just launched upon their technical training. Some were still in high school, and only a few of them had completed their engineering training. Nevertheless, they plunged with zeal into the task of introducing Western technology into China. Often their efforts were met with disdain and sometimes with outright hostility. But a high sense of duty kept them to their task, and with scarcely any exceptions they refused to be tempted away from the service of the Government to the more lucrative private enterprises around them. For years they worked in obscurity as telegraph operators, railroad and mine foremen. Some few served as technical officers in China's navy. Eventually their value to the emerging new China could no longer be denied and they rose to positions more in keeping with their abilities. Some became cabinet members and even prime ministers. Others ended their careers as admirals or diplomats. All were tremendously influential in initiating China into the arts of shipbuilding and railroad and mining development. In fact, one finds them supplying the initiative and skill in every undertaking of this character upon which the Chinese Government embarked prior to 1900. After 1900, the folly of the Boxer Rebellion opened China to the foreign concessionnaire, who eagerly availed himself of the opportunities thus offered. The result was that the earlier work of the former students of the Educational Mission tended to become obscured, and the illusion arose that the introduction of railroads, telegraphs, and mining into China was accomplished solely by the enterprise and initiative of foreigners. Such was certainly not the case, for the ground had been well prepared by this small band of pioneer engineers who had amply demonstrated the ability of the Chinese to absorb and apply the technical knowledge of the West.

In the following pages I have attempted to trace the part these men played in the emergence of the China of today. Justice demands that honor be placed where honor is due. The modernization of China was not brought about by the few Occidental diplomats, merchants, and engineers who figure so prominently in Occidental histories of the Far East. Actually the Chinese upon their own initiative launched almost all the positive moves towards modernization. In fact, it can be truly said that after 1900, when China was opened up to foreign railroad and mining enterprise, the jealousies and bickerings of the Occidental nations actually retarded the building of railroads and the development of mines. Perhaps this slight volume will in a measure correct a picture which has been painted almost entirely from the Western viewpoint. The Chinese are a remarkable people and quite capable of determining their own destiny. It has taken their magnificent resistance to a brutal assault upon their freedom and independence to make the West realize this simple truth. They ask favors of no one. All they demand is the right to live and develop in freedom and independence. May the following pages throw light upon the activities of a small group of men who did much to prepare the way for the Free China of today .

It is with deep pleasure that I extend my heartfelt gratitude first to the few remaining survivors of the Chinese Educational Mission to the United States who so graciously entertained me in their homes and aided me on my visit to China in the summer of 1940. Secondly, I should like to thank Mr. Arthur G. Robinson, who with great generosity passed on to me the materials on the Mission which he had painstakingly collected over the great number of years he was a resident in China. I should like to thank Professor L. C. Goodrich of Columbia University who has been ever ready with suggestions and precious bits of information. To the Social Science Research Council and to the American Council of Learned Societies I express my gratitude for their part in enabling me to pursue my inquiries in China.

Finally, I should like to extend my thanks to President E. O. Holland of the State College of Washington for his sustained interest in this study and for making it possible to have it published by the Press of the State College of Washington.

Thomas E. LaFargue

Pullman, Washington, February 3, 1942.

China's First Hundred

CHAPTER I

MANDARINS AND MACHINES

When Marco Polo whiled away the tedium of his Genoese prison by recounting to his fellow prisoners tales of his adventures in the rich and fabulous countries of the East, he fired the imaginations of generations of Europeans with dreams of quick and easy wealth to be won from the effete and unwarlike peoples of the Orient. Inspired by his tales, countless adventurers were drawn to the shores of China and to the islands of the Indies. Here, merchant, soldier, and priest,—each hoped to garner his own rich harvest. The Indies, parcelled out among a score of petty sultans, soon fell under the sway of the European; but China, intensely loyal to her emperor and proud of an age-old culture, remained indifferent to the "red-haired barbarians" chaffering and clamouring at the southern-most corner of her empire. Confined as they were to the single port of Canton, these strangers from across the sea had little opportunity to influence or be influenced by the Chinese.

It was far different, however, with the coming of the nineteenth century. Now the overwhelming impact of the machine power civilization of the Occident gave the West possession of weapons powerful enough to fashion the whole world after its own image. A highly developed technology enlisted in the service of an aggressive nationalism and an ever expanding industrial system proved more powerful than all the invasions of the past to change the ancient patterns of Chinese life.

The conviction of Europeans that it was their Christian duty and the manifest destiny of the people of the Occident to bring to China the fruits of western civilization was accepted without question. Typical of all western thinking was the view expressed by Mr. F. S. Seward, the United States Consul at Shanghai, when he wrote apropos of some foreigners who had

1

erected a telegraph line against the protests of the Chinese Government:

> "I confess that I should think less of western civilization and of western manhood if it were not pushing and aggressive in China. Take the average American or Englishman used to well-kept roads and streets, to well-policed towns, to the comforts and conveniences, and advantages of steamships, telegraphs, and railroads. . . and put him down in China where there is not one carriage road; where there are no sewers nor lamps in the towns; where telegraphs and railroads are unknown, and steamers only where foreigners have forced them. . . and he would be unworthy of the Anglo-Saxon blood which runs in his veins if he should teach himself the Chinese habit of thought, and sit down to believe with the immobile mass around him that whatever is, is best."

The enthusiasm of the aggressive foreigners for bringing the mechanistic aspects of Occidental civilization to China was met by a determination upon the part of the Confucian officials to resist the introduction of the steamship, the railroad, and the telegraph, for they immediately recognized that if these powerful instrumentalities of Western machine civilization once became established in China, the foundations of China's agricultural and handicraft culture would be rapidly undermined. Moreover, the all-powerful scholar officials, whose monopoly of the administration of China depended upon a universal acceptance of the teachings of Confucius as the basis of government, perceived that the technology of the West threatened their control of the Imperial government. Yet a handful of China's wiser statesmen saw that the time had come when China could no longer play the proud role of the "Middle Kingdom", overawing with the sheer superiority of her culture a circle of admiring satellite states. They realized that new and irresistible forces were playing upon their ancient civilization and that if it were to be preserved, China would have to arm herself with the same weapons with which the Occidental nations were threatening to dismember her. At first with hesitation but later with increasing confidence, these few statesmen took steps to provide China with a modern army and navy and to train young Chinese in the network of professions upon which the effectiveness of modern armies and navies depends.

Only in this restricted sense can these early advocates of the introduction of Western technology into China be considered reformers. None of them seemed ever to have developed a genuine admiration for the machine technology of the Occident. Their only object was to place China in a position where the ever-increasing pressure from the West could be resisted so that, protected by a strong army and navy, China could pursue the even tenor of her age-old ways.

The introduction of Western technology into China is associated almost exclusively with the names of a few great officials. For the most part they were governors and viceroys of the coastal provinces, men who had ample opportunity to observe the striking power of modern weapons of warfare when China first clashed with Great Britain and France in the Opium Wars of 1840 and 1856. Foremost among this small group was Tsêng Kuo-fan, an obscure provincial official whom the great T'ai P'ing rebellion of the middle nineteenth century brought to the fore as the commander of the Imperial armies. The rebellion, which ranged from 1850 to 1865, came within an ace of overthrowing the Manchu dynasty; but finally the rebels were crushed and their various strongholds captured and destroyed. In the closing phases of the campaign, Tsêng employed numerous foreigners to assist him in putting down the rebellion. Among these was General Charles Gordon who organized a group of foreigners into a highly disciplined army. This force won so many victories over the T'ai P'ings that the Chinese called it the "Ever Victorious Army". Another adventurer who took service under the Manchus was Frederick Ward, the son of a Salem sea captain turned soldier of fortune. A valiant and reckless fighter, he was ambushed and killed by the T'ai P'ings. To honor his memory the Chinese buried him in a Confucian temple and erected a small shrine before his grave.

As commander of the Imperial forces, Tsêng Kuo-fan was greatly impressed by the discipline and effectiveness of these foreign mercenaries. He immediately perceived the immense advantages enjoyed by a body of soldiers armed with modern rifles and artillery and obedient to the military discipline characteristic of Occidental armies. During the course of the rebellion, Tsêng bought some foreign steam vessels to transport and to protect his troops. These vessels were antiquated ships which some foreigners had hastily armed and palmed off on the Chinese, but against such armor-protected vessels the junks of the rebels were no more effective than chaff thrown in the wind. Tsêng resolved that the wooden war junks of China and her undisciplined legions armed largely with spears and bows would have to go. Therefore, immediately after peace was restored, he began to memorialize the Throne asking permission to employ numerous foreign experts to teach the Chinese the secrets of Occidental military might. He also advocated the establishment of dock yards and arsenals so that China could become independent of foreign sources for her war materials.

Tsêng Kuo-fan was ably supported in his advocacy of the modernization of China's army and navy by his great lieutenant, Li Hung-chang. The T'ai P'ing rebellion had also given Li the opportunity to display his extraordinary talents, and when it ended in 1865, he and Tsêng Kuo-fan enjoyed the highest Imperial favor. In the next few years these two, together with a few other "reforming officials", started China along the road of westernization. They built dockyards and arsenals in which

4

were constructed China's first modern ships of war and artillery. Attached to these establishments and forming a vital part of them were training schools in which a number of young Chinese, under the supervision of foreign teachers, were initiated into the mysteries of shipbuilding, engineering, and numerous other technical crafts. Tsêng died in 1871 and thereafter Li Hung-chang dominated Chinese politics until in 1895 the disgrace of China's defeat in the Sino-Japanese war forced him into retirement. During his period of power Li was back of every scheme to introduce into China railroads and telegraphs and to organize steamship lines so that the Chinese could compete with the foreigners for the vast coastal and river commerce of China.

Another Chinese statesman whom the troubled conditions of nineteenth century China brought to the fore was Tso Tsung-t'ang. Tso's interest in western armaments had been first aroused during the Opium War of 1840-1842. In this war he witnessed the disastrous effects upon the poorly-equipped Chinese troops of the artillery and rifle fire of the British regiments. The defeat suffered by China served only to quicken the interest of Tso Tsung-t'ang in modern methods of warfare. He devoted a great deal of time to the problem of coastal defense, and when the T'ai P'ing rebellion arose in 1850, he began to put into practice some of his ideas for equipping the Imperial armies with adequate armaments. As early as 1852 he submitted a plan to the Imperial Court for the creation of a navy armed with modern guns. In 1854 we find him actively engaged in casting guns and building ships at Hui-Ch'eng, where the governor of Hunan had established an arsenal. Tso is credited with inventing the P'i Shan P'ao or Splitting Mountain Gun, and with casting over a hundred of these weapons. During the last years of the T'ai P'ing insurrection, he had several opportunities to see in action the foreign legions which had been enlisted under the Imperial banner.

Again he was impressed with the utter helplessness of troops equipped with antiquated Chinese arms in the face of

5

Western methods of warfare. In 1865 at the end of the rebellion Tso was appointed Viceroy of the coastal provinces of Chekiang and Fukien. This was an ideal situation in which he might begin to create a modern Chinese navy. At first he was content to charter foreign vessels and to employ foreign crews, but what he really wanted was to establish a dockyard and to build his own war vessels. In 1864, he constructed a small steamer and experimented with it on the West Lake at Hangchow. Finally, in 1866, Tso received Imperial sanction to establish an arsenal and dockyard at Foochow on the Fukien coast. To carry out this enterprise he engaged a French engineer, Prosper Giquel. Giquel was one of the many foreigners who had been drawn to China by the prospects of adventure and lucrative employment. During the T'ai P'ing rebellion he had been commissioned by the Imperial Government to form a Franco-Chinese corps to sweep the area around Shanghai clear of rebels. It was while he was engaged in this task that he came to the notice of Tso Tsung-t'ang.

Giquel was an extremely competent engineer, and in a short while he had designed and constructed an extensive engineering and shipbuilding plant at Foochow. Once the dockyard had been completed, he embarked upon an ambitious program to construct a series of war vessels. At the same time he began to train a considerable body of Chinese in the mechanical and technical skills connected with the building of ships and the design and construction of machinery. The prejudice of the Chinese towards this "barbarian" undertaking was such that it was actually necessary to attract apprentices by paying them as much as the salary of a clerk in a government office. The experiment soon justified whatever it cost, for by 1874 there had been launched from the shipbuilding yard at Foochow fifteen small steamers. Moreover a considerable body of Chinese workmen had received a great deal of practical experience in the operation of machinery and the construction of modern steam vessels.

In 1869, before the arsenal at Foochow was fully completed, Tso was ordered to proceed to the northwest provinces of Kansu and Shensi to suppress a great rebellion of the Mohammedan population in these provinces. Tso realized that if he were to depend upon the old-fashioned Chinese methods of warfare, the suppression of this rebellion would be a long and hazardous task. He resolved to use modern artillery and rifles against the rebels, and in order to overcome the difficulties of transporting them into the interior, he took with him to Kansu a number of Chinese mechanics who had gained some knowledge of the manufacture of Western arms at such places as Foochow and Canton. With their aid Tso constructed a small arsenal at Lanchow and, in addition, he built the first woolen mill in China to be operated by machinery to supply the uniforms for his troops.

After the successful suppression of the rebellion, Tso continued to interest himself in Western technology. Unlike some of the other reformers among his fellow officials, he had ideas which went beyond the mere strengthening of China against Occidental aggression. He realized that the introduction of modern means of transportation would solve some of the economic problems which had given rise to the T'ai P'ing and the Mohammedan rebellions.

No reference can be made to the modernization of China without mentioning the name of Chang Chih-tung. Chang was born in 1837 of a family which for generations had belonged to the official class. His father was chief magistrate of Kueichou and his elder brother attained the most coveted distinction in the Chinese empire by taking first place in the triennial Metropolitan examinations. In 1863, when Chang took the Metropolitan examinations, he surprised his examiners and gave evidence of his independence of character and the progressiveness of his outlook by choosing to write his essay upon the T'ai P'ing rebellion and similar current topics rather than upon the customary themes taken from the Confucian classics. This act of daring brought him to the attention of the Grand Secretary, Pao Yun, who had Chang's paper placed in the first group of successful candidates. His official career thus assured, he entered with zest into the great game of Chinese politics. He occupied a series of increasingly important posts and in 1881 was appointed governor of Shansi province. When Chang arrived to take up his duties, he found the province undergoing a severe famine. The sufferings of the people were greatly increased by the rapaciousness of a group of dishonest officials who were using the famine as an excuse to raise the price of grain. In taking measures to correct this immediate situation, Chang soon found himself launched upon the path of reform. He realized that the famine in Shansi was largely due to the lack of adequate transportation whereby the grain could be moved from one province to another. Before he had time to formulate proposals for an improvement of inland transportation, war broke out between China and France over the control of Tonking. Chang now became intensely interested in schemes for strengthening the Chinese army and for creating a navy so that China's southern border could be protected against French aggression. He submitted a series of memorials to the Throne in which he proposed drastic changes in the arms and discipline of the Imperial forces. As a result of these suggestions, in 1884 he was made Viceroy of Kuangtung and Kuangsi, and the defense of the southern border was placed in his hands. He arrived in the South too late to do much against the French as in 1885 the diplomats in Peking settled the Tonking question. However, before the close of the war he gained considerable fame by an unexpected victory over the French forces at the battle of Langson. In spite of this victory, Tonking was lost to China and fell under the control of France. Chang was not discouraged by these events and he devoted himself more than ever to the problem of coastal defense. In 1886 he prepared and presented to the Court a treatise on this subject. He also established at

8

Canton a dockyard and naval college patterned after the one set up by Tso Tsung-t'ang at Foochow. While at Canton he became very much interested in currency reform and built a mint in order to make a uniform coinage to replace the haphazard varieties of local currency then in use.

In 1889 Chang was made Viceroy of the Yangtze Valley provinces of Hupeh and Hunan. Soon after occupying this post, he presented to the Throne a project for a great trunk railway to connect North China with the Yangtze Valley at Hankow. This proposal arose out of Chang's earlier experiences in Shansi, when he had realized that the lack of transportation to move grain from province to province was the basic cause for famines in China. Chang also wanted to make a counter-move against his political rival, Li Hung-chang, under whose patronage a short railway had been built in Chihli province north of Tientsin. Li now proposed to make this line a real trunk railway by extending it to Tientsin in the south and to Shanhaikuan in the north. Chang Chih-tung opposed such an extension on the ground that railways along the coast in time of war would enable the enemy to gain access to the capital. In its place he brought forward his plan for a series of trunk railways to be built in the interior where they would be comparatively safe from seizure by an invading army. Favorably impressed by his arguments, the Court gave him the task of constructing a railway between Peking and Hankow. However, he progressed no further in this project than to build an iron and steel plant to manufacture the rails. In the meantime, the effect of his proposal was to get Li Hung-chang's railway schemes temporarily shelved. The iron and steel plant grew into the great Han Yeh P'ing foundry at Hanyang on the middle Yangtze. In later years there grew up around this plant the industrial center of China, and Hanyang became known as the "Chicago of China".

In military affairs Chang leaned towards German and Japanese methods. He employed a considerable number of Ger-

9

man military instructors to train his provincial troops and, after the Sino-Japanese war of 1895, he purchased several naval craft from Japan and encouraged young Chinese to go there to study. In 1898, however, when the Emperor Kuang Hsü launched upon a wholesale series of reforms, Chang Chih-tung, despite his desire for modernization, drew back and threw his support to the conservative Empress Dowager.

After the Boxer uprising of 1900, which Chang successfully weathered, he turned his attention to plans for a modern system of education. It was his belief that reform in China should be brought about gradually as a result of education rather than violently as a result of revolution. In 1903 he participated in inaugurating a system of schools in which students would be given a knowledge of science, mathematics, and other technical subjects. He died in 1909 while still at the peak of his influence and favor with the Manchu Court.

Finally in this group of reformers we come to the inheritor of all of his predecessors' efforts to lead China along the path of westernization. This was Yüan Shih-k'ai, the man who truly stood between the old imperial China of the nineteenth century and the republican China of the twentieth century. His position between two totally different worlds, the world of old Confucian China and the new world of steamships, railroads, and modern armies, and battleships, made him confused in his aims. He spent his life equipping the Chinese army with modern weapons and in persuading a reluctant Court to turn its face towards political reform, but he died involved in the midst of China's oldest political trick, the attempt to establish himself upon the dragon throne as the founder of a new dynasty. Yüan represented a younger generation of reformers than that of Tsêng Kuo-fan, Li Hung-chang, Tso Tsung-t'ang and Chang Chih-tung. He was born in 1860 just when the T'ai P'ing rebellion was finally being suppressed. He first came into prominence in 1884 when he was sent as Chinese Resident to

Korea, which by this time had become the battleground of the political rivalry between Japan and China. Yüan's job was to keep Korea under the domination of Peking rather than to let it slip under Japanese control. He was so successful in accomplishing this task that until the outbreak of the Sino-Japanese war in 1894, he virtually ruled Korea. In fact, it was Yüan's domination of Korean affairs that caused Japan to resort to a war to overcome Chinese influence in Korea. In 1894, upon the outbreak of hostilities between China and Japan, Yüan returned to Peking. The subsequent defeat of China in the war caused his patron, Li Hung-chang, to fall into disgrace; but contrary to the usual practice whereby a subordinate also suffers for the mistakes of his chief, Yüan survived the war and soon became recognized as the logical successor to Li Hung-chang as the foremost exponent of modernization. He was first placed in charge of the foreign drilled troops of Chihli province, and by his vigorous methods and severe discipline, he soon had at his disposal a thoroughly efficient and properly equipped force.

In 1898, at the time of the Hundred Days' Reforms, when the young Emperor, Kuang Hsü, attempted to modernize China almost overnight, Yüan Shih-k'ai followed Chang Chih-tung in opposing the emperor. He actively aided the Empress Dowager, the aunt of the emperor, to seize control of the government and to imprison the emperor. In this instance, Yüan betrayed the reform movement which he considered to be too hastily conceived. At the same time he earned the deep gratitude of the Empress Dowager, and until her death in 1908 he was her most trusted advisor.

Upon the death of Li Hung-chang in 1901, Yüan Shih-k'ai succeeded Li as Viceroy of Chihli province. This was the most important of all the vice-royalties as it contained the capital and seat of Imperial government. To be appointed to the vice-royalty of Chihli was the highest mark of Imperial trust and favor. It raised Yüan to the pinnacle of power and from 1901 to 1908, when his enemies succeeded in forcing him into retirement, he was the most influential official in the Chinese empire. It was during his tenure of power that China was launched upon the path of constitutional government and a modern system of education was established.

When the Empress Dowager died in 1908, Yüan lost his protector. His enemies, who had never forgotten the part he had played in 1898 in betraying the young emperor into the hands of the Empress Dowager, drove him from official life. He retired to his farm in Honan. The outbreak of the revolution in 1911 found him living the life of the simple farmer. Once again the Manchus turned to him to save the dynasty, but now he betrayed his trust by bringing about the abdication of the dynasty to make way for the Republic. The part he played in the formation of the Republic and the confusion of his last years will be treated in a later chapter. He was typical of his times. Caught between the old and the new China he constantly attempted to find a balance between hopelessly opposed forces. He failed and in 1915 he died distrusted by the conservatives and the reformers alike.

Fascinating as such a story might be, I do not propose to write about these great figures in the drama of Nineteenth Century Chinese history. They were the policy makers and without their aid and patronage, the more humble figures in the drama, the men with whom we are primarily concerned in the following pages, would never have had the opportunity to be educated in the United States nor upon their return to China to have been able to put into practice the technical knowledge they had acquired while abroad. These were the men who were actually entrusted with the task of carrying out the plans of the great officials mentioned above. They were drawn from a group of one hundred and twenty young Chinese youths who between 1872 and 1874 were sent to the United States to be thoroughly educated in the various technical professions intimately connected with the arts of war. The plan for their education, usually referred to as the Chinese Educational Mission to the United States, was launched under the patronage of Tsêng Kuo-fan and Li Hung-chang. The project had the sanction of the Imperial Government, but the responsibility for its success or failure was left to these two officials.

In substance, the plan was to send to the United States annual contingents of thirty carefully selected Chinese youths between the ages of twelve and sixteen. They were to remain in the United States for fifteen years. At the end of that time, they were to return to China and to spend their lives in the service of the Government. It was hoped that by this method the Imperial Government would have at its disposal a constantly growing body of technically trained engineers who would be able to build railroads, erect telegraph lines, construct warships, and manufacture guns and ammunitions. By using this ever growing body of native engineers, the necessity of farming out such enterprises to foreign concessionaires could be avoided. Moreover, foreigners would be kept at a distance while China was arming herself with the technical paraphernalia of Occidental military and naval might.

The Mission was launched while China was still smarting from the humiliating defeat she had suffered at the hands of the French and English during the war of 1856-60. All patriotic Chinese statesmen had been profoundly shocked by this defeat and many of them realized that China, armed with her antiquated weapons and without any system of transportation for the quick movement of troops, was at the mercy of any aggressive Occidental nation which cared to attack her. Aroused by China's plight a few of the viceroys in the coastal provinces had built dockyards and arsenals in an attempt to put China in a better position to defend herself, but the effectiveness of these institutions depended almost entirely upon the active and continuing support of the later viceroys who succeeded these early innovators. By long tradition the defense of the coast was looked upon as the concern of the governors of the coastal provinces rather than of the Imperial Government in Peking.

The lessons of the wars of 1840 and 1856 were soon forgotten, however, and a conservative reaction set in, causing the advocates of westernization to become unpopular at Court. This was particularly true after 1880 when the Empress Dowager, Tz'u Hsi, began to dominate the Government. After the death of Tsêng Kuo-fan, in 1871, the Conservatives gradually came back into favor. They despised the Educational Mission, in which they saw a bowing down to the power of the hated foreigners. Moreover, to attack it was an easy way to attack Li Hung-chang, whom the Conservatives disliked and wished to disgrace. By 1881 they were able to engineer the abolition of the Mission; and the students, some one hundred in all, were suddenly recalled in the midst of their studies. Through the efforts of Li Hung-chang, attempts were made to finish their training in the arsenals and dockyards which had been set up in China, but such institutions could offer them only practical instructions in the management and operation of machinery, guns, etc. They could not be given the scientific and theoretical instruction which lies at the basis of all the advanced professions. Thus, the students of the Missions were handicapped at the very start by the incomplete nature of their training.

Furthermore, when the students first returned to China, they were treated as if their long residence in America had unfitted them for rendering any service to their homeland. The Confucian scholars, who made up the official class, looked upon them as only a little above coolies. To treat them as equals was unthinkable. Nevertheless, from this pioneer group there emerged China's first engineers, railway builders, telegraph builders, mining experts, and technical officers in her new navy. A few of them eventually rose to positions of great prominence, but for the most part they remained in humble posts as far as official rank was concerned. Their claim to be remembered rests upon their collective efforts to introduce the technical sciences into China rather than upon the brilliant careers of the few famous ones among them.

The official class never overcame its hostility toward these students who departed so markedly both in their training and attitude from the conventional ideal of a Confucian scholar. In fact, the difficulties which the students of the Educational Mission encountered when they returned to China reflected China's first reactions to the impact of Western civilization. China did not accept with any pleasure the technological gifts which the West was only too ready to force upon her. The initial impulse of the Confucian mandarinate was to resist any penetration into China of western science. When two wars demonstrated that the military and naval power of the West could not be resisted by the time-honored weapons of defense, a few of the mandarins set themselves to discover the secret of the aggressive military power of the European nations. Having discovered this secret, their next thought was to arm China with modern arms and battleships. It was in this phase of westernization that most of the former students of the Mission spent their lives. In this light their lives take on more than a personal significance. In fact, we are not only viewing here the personal experiences of a small group of Chinese whom Fate had called upon to put into practice the projects of such reforming Viceroys as Tsêng Kuo-fan and Li Hung-chang, but through their lives we catch glimpses at the very point of contact of the conflict between the philosophical, stable, repetitive civilization of old China and the materialistic, changing, aggressive civilization of the 19th century Occident.

After 1900, the reform movement in China became a genuine movement to change the political and economic milieu of the Chinese people. Not only were the technological instruments of Occidental civilization welcomed, but the educational and political institutions, which in the Occident gave the sciences such broad significance, were gradually adopted by China. But by this time a whole new generation of returned students were eager to take over this revolutionary task. After the Revolution of 1911, they were able to shoulder the 19th century "westernizers" out of the way as being old-fashioned in their technical training. Moreover, their long service under the Manchu regime made them politically suspect in the eyes of the young republicans. A few of them were prominent in the first years of the Republic, but once they had served as convenient tools for the republicans or for the monarchical schemes of Yüan Shih-k'ai, they soon disappeared from public life. After 1915 most of them fade into the obscurity of retirement. A small handful of the original one hundred and twenty now live in the port cities, forgotten in the desperate struggle for freedom which China is now undergoing. It is hoped that this record will serve as a memorial to this small group of Chinese who loyally served their country in a most difficult time of transition. They not only saw the emergence of a "new China"; they prepared the way.

CHAPTER II

YUNG WING: THE FORERUNNER

On November 17, 1828, there was born in the small and obscure village of Nam Ping in South China a Chinese boy whose name was Yung Wing. His life mirrored the experience of the Chinese nation as it emerged from its old Confucian chrysalis to the new China of today. Above everything, Yung Wing was a forerunner. He was the first Chinese in modern times to break completely away from the age-old Chinese social environment and to divorce himself from the cultural inheritance of his people. He marks an important point in the history of his country, for from him there stems in an ever widening stream that numerous body of young Chinese who, first in the mission schools in China and later in the colleges and universities of Europe and the United States, have become thoroughly imbued with the "western viewpoint" and who have consciously striven to spread this viewpoint among their own people. He was the first and the most typical of that peculiar Chinese type, "the returned student."

Yung Wing was the second son of a family of four children. His parents were typical peasant people of the region, engaged primarily in farming but also interested in various business enterprises connected with their village. Nam Ping is situated on Pedro Island, a small point of land two miles or so off shore from the old historic Portuguese trading post of Macao and some ninety miles from the great port of Canton. The close association of the villagers with the foreign trade of the Canton region and the proximity of the Portuguese settlement had long worn away their traditional suspicion of anything connected with the "western barbarians." In fact, Yung Wing's parents were only too anxious to have their son form some connection with the foreign community at Canton, so that later he might become a clerk in a foreign hong or trading establishment. By good fortune one of the neighbors of the Yung family was the chief servant for the Reverend Charles Gutzlaff and his wife, missionaries at Macao. Mrs. Gutzlaff, an energetic and capable woman, had long been interested in establishing a school for girls at Macao, and in the summer of 1835 she succeeded in opening such a school.

About the same time the foreign community in Canton decided to establish the Morrison Educational Society in memory of Robert Morrison, the first Protestant missionary to China. The purpose of the society, as set forth in a circular inviting subscriptions, was to establish schools "in which native youth shall be taught, in connection with their own, to read and write the English language; and through this medium to bring within their reach all the varied learning of the western world." Pending the actual establishment of a school by the Morrison Society, a few very young boys were admitted to Mrs. Gutzlaff's girls' school. Through the influence of the Gutzlaff's servant from Nam Ping, Yung Wing was one of the small boys so admitted. Thus, in this fortuitous manner there began the career of the first Chinese ever to receive a thorough Occidental education. The very uniqueness of his experiences filled his life with difficulties, for quite naturally his fellow-countrymen looked with suspicion on one who had the temerity to break so decisively with the social mores of old China. Yung Wing, and those who followed him, could expect little appreciation of their western knowledge from their compatriots. They were objects of suspicion and only slowly, as the forces of Western civilization crept into China, did they find their place in the changing Chinese environment.

What were the feelings of this young Chinese lad when, at the age of seven, he found himself in the presence of Mrs. Gutzlaff, the first foreign lady he had ever seen? She was a large and well-proportioned Saxon type with fair hair and blue eyes.

It was summer, and Mrs. Gutzlaff wore a long white flowing dress with large globe-like sleeves. Yung Wing relates that he trembled all over with fear at this first encounter, for her appearance was terrifying to him. But it did not take long for him to be quite won over by the kindness of Mrs. Gutzlaff. Under her matronly care, he received his first introduction to western learning.

By 1839 the Morrison Educational Society had succeeded in establishing a boys school at Macao and had secured as headmaster for the school the Reverend Samuel Robbins Brown. He had been educated at Yale and came highly recommended by the authorities of the College. In the meantime, Yung Wing's father had died, leaving the support of the family up to him and his elder brother. For a short time Yung Wing worked in the printing office of a Catholic priest but through the aid of Dr. Benjamin Hobson, a medical missionary, in 1841 he enrolled in the Morrison School. There Yung Wing found five other Chinese lads who had already been in the school one year. They were Wong Hsing, Wong Foon, Li Kan, Chow Wan and Tong Chik. So difficult was it to induce the Chinese to send their sons to the foreign school that at least two of these young boys had been picked up on the streets of Canton as homeless outcasts and the parents of the others had to be paid in order to consent to have their sons placed in the charge of foreigners. Yet most of these lads had distinguished careers and more than fulfilled the hopes of the promoters of the school by serving as pioneers in bringing western arts and civilization to China. Wong Foon became China's first western trained physician and led a long and useful career in introducing western medicine to his fellow countrymen. Wong Hsing remained a teacher and, many years later, when Yung Wing had persuaded the Chinese Government to send a group of young Chinese to be educated in the schools of the United States, he accompanied the students to act as an interpreter and teacher to them. Tong Chik, better known as Tong King-sing, became a famous business man. He had the distinction of forming China's first steamship company, the China Merchants Steam Navigation Company. He also inspired the building of China's first native-built railroad and the development of China's first modern coal mines. Another of the pupils was employed in the office of Governor Lin Tse-hsü, the imperial commissioner sent to Canton in 1839 by the emperor to suppress the opium traffic. It was Lin who seized and burned the opium of the British merchants, thus bringing on the first Anglo-Chinese war. Despite Lin's determination to stamp out the opium traffic, he was greatly interested in the foreigners and he inveigled away one of the Morrison school pupils to aid him in translating English papers and books about the nations of the West. Much of this material was incorporated in Wei Yuan's *Hai Kuo T'u Chih,* the *Description of the Maritime Nations.* This work, published in 1844, was the first attempt of a Chinese mandarin to inform his fellow officials about the western world.

In 1847, ill health compelled Samuel Robbins Brown, principal of the Morrison school, to return to the United States. When he was ready to leave he invited volunteers from among his students to return with him in order that they might complete their education. Wong Hsing, Wong Foon and Yung Wing eagerly availed themselves of this opportunity and, on the 4th of January, 1847, they left Canton aboard the Olyphant Brothers' ship, the "Huntress", bound for New York. The money to defray the expenses of these three lads was supplied by popular subscription from among the foreign residents at Canton. Upon landing in New York, the lads had their first meeting with Professor David E. Bartlett and his wife. From this initial introduction, the Bartletts became intimately connected with the movement to educate Chinese students in America and, later in the 1870's, their house in Hartford, Connecticut became the home of many of the students sent to America in the charge of Yung Wing. From New York Yung

Wing and his companions were sent to the Monson Academy in Monson, Massachusetts.

Because of ill-health, Wong Hsing soon returned to China, but Yung Wing and Wong Foon remained, being graduated from the Academy in 1849. Both boys were very desirous of entering Yale College, but the patrons in Canton who had enabled them to go abroad had provided for only two years' stay in America. If the young men would have promised to become missionaries, funds could easily have been obtained from American Church societies to defray the cost of further education. Neither, however, felt any call in this direction. Finally, Andrew Shortrede, proprietor of the Hong Kong *China Mail,* wrote them that he would furnish funds for their education if they would go to the University of Edinburgh to study medicine. Shortrede was a patriotic Scotchman, and he wanted Scotland to have the honor of training the first Chinese to become physicians. Wong Foon decided to accept this offer and he departed for Scotland. He finished his medical studies in 1855 and then returned to China. For many years he was in charge of the London Mission Hospital at Canton and thus was able to render great service to his countrymen. Among foreigners and Chinese alike he was recognized as one of the most skilled surgeons on the China coast. He died in 1878.

Wong Hsing, who had been forced to return to China because of ill-health, learned the art of printing in the office of the *China Mail.* He also was connected with the press of the London Missionary Society and aided Dr. James Legge in his translations of the Chinese classics. We shall see that he eventually returned to the United States in charge of one of the groups of Chinese youths who were sent to America by the Chinese Government in 1872.

Yung Wing could not bring himself to forsake America for Scotland, neither did he want to pledge himself to become a missionary. Either course would have given him the funds necessary to complete his education, but he had resolved to keep himself free from any obligations so that when he returned to China he would be able to avail himself of whatever opportunities that might arise to serve his people. In the midst of his perplexities, he was greatly encouraged by a small sum sent to him by "The Ladies Association of Savannah, Ga.", who had heard of him through his friend and teacher, the Reverend Samuel Robbins Brown. Thus heartened, he went down to New Haven to take the entrance examinations for Yale College. He was admitted, although his preparation was far behind that of his fellow students. By dint of constant application, however, he soon overcame his initial handicaps and thereafter was recognized as one of the outstanding students of his class.

The financial difficulties, which had loomed so large in his imagination, also soon disappeared before his determination. As many an American youth had done before him, he earned his room and board by becoming student manager of a boarding club. He did all the marketing for the club and waited on table. In his sophomore year he won the first prize in English composition on two occasions. This distinction led to his being appointed assistant librarian to the Brothers in Unity, one of the important literary societies at Yale College. The Ladies Association in Savannah continued to take an interest in him and sent him occasional gifts of money, together with socks, shirts, and other articles of clothing.

Yung Wing's career at Yale was successful. He was well known and very much liked among his classmates. He seems to have had a facility for absorbing his American environment and when he left Yale, in 1854, he was thoroughly Americanized. In fact, in 1852 he had become a naturalized American citizen.

During his four years at Yale he had thought much concerning the future of China and the role he might be able to play in preparing China to take her proper place in the modern world. He became convinced that China's only hope was to scrap her ancient philosophical civilization and adopt as rapidly as possible the technological, progressive civilization of the Occident. He believed that this could best be done by the Chinese Government sending abroad a constant stream of carefully selected Chinese youths to be educated in the schools of America and Europe. From the very beginning, it was Yung Wing's idea that these youths should remain in America or Europe for a period sufficiently long to give them a thorough Occidental education, so that they would deeply absorb the "western viewpoint." In fact, he wanted to de-chinese them as much as possible, for he felt that only by such a thorough process of inculcation would these youths be able to overcome the tremendous difficulties of introducing into the hostile Chinese environment the technology and machinery of the West. Although the conception was too bold to be completely successful, after many years of frustration Yung Wing actually succeeded in getting such a project launched. In the Chinese Educational Mission to the United States he was able to achieve in a high measure the realization of his hopes.

In 1854, when Yung Wing returned to China, he found little to encourage him in his plan to westernize the empire. The great T'ai P'ing rebellion was raging and it seemed only a matter of time before the decadent Manchu regime would be overthrown. The T'ai P'ing rebels had succeeded in enveloping their movement with a pseudo Christian character which their acts of cruelty and misgovernment soon betrayed. In 1859 Yung Wing made a trip to the T'ai P'ing headquarters at Nanking in order to ascertain the character of the T'ai P'ing leaders, but any illusions which he might have had that the rebellion would lead to the salvation of China were dispelled by what he was able to observe at first hand. Thereafter, he sought among the imperial officials for some one who would be willing to aid him in the realization of his plans.

The T'ai P'ing rebellion was indirectly the means whereby Yung Wing was able to make a modest fortune which placed him beyond the necessity of offering his services to whoever cared to make use of them. Because the interior provinces were held by the T'ai P'ings and the coastal cities were controlled by the Imperialists the trade between the two areas languished. This was especially true of the tea trade. In the T'ai P'ing districts millions of pounds of tea accumulated in the warehouses with little likelihood of ever getting it to the market. Yung Wing, attracted by the adventure and by the opportunity to make a quick fortune, volunteered to go into the tea districts to get out some of the tea impounded there by the T'ai P'ings. His proposal was taken up by some of the tea firms in Shanghai and, within six months, Yung Wing succeeded in bringing out several thousand pounds of tea. With the profit acquired from the venture he was able to go into the tea business on his own account and in a few years he became moderately rich.

The life of a wealthy merchant, however, held no permanent charms for him. He had never lost sight of his plan to induce the Chinese Government to embark upon a program of educating Chinese youths in the institutions of the Occident. He had no influence of his own to bring such a project to the attention of the Chinese Government. What he needed was access to some powerful mandarin who would favor such a scheme and who would be willing to propose it in a memorial to the Throne.

In the end, the very disorder into which China had fallen worked to further Yung Wing's plans. The great T'ai P'ing rebellion brought to the fore resolute men, very different from the usual time-serving mandarin type. Among such resolute men, none was more powerful and prominent than Tsêng Kuo-fan. The necessities of the times had drawn Tsêng from an obscure provincial post to become the commander of all the Imperial forces. Through his skill and energy the rebellion was finally suppressed and the Manchu dynasty was given a new lease of power. Mention has already been made of the fact that in the course of the rebellion, Tsêng employed armed steam vessels to transport his troops and to destroy the war junks of the T'ai P'ings and that he enlisted a considerable body of western adventurers, who, with their superior arms and under the capable leadership of General Charles "Chinese" Gordon, contributed quite materially to the eventual victory of the Imperial forces.

Tsêng was thoroughly converted to the use of Western arms, and once the rebellion was suppressed and order restored he took up the task of modernizing China's army and creating a navy. At the same time that Yung Wing was searching for some powerful official who would take up his educational project, Tsêng was looking for someone who was acquainted with the West and who would aid him in procuring machinery for the arsenal and dockyard he was planning to build. The mutual interests of the two men soon brought them together.

At the conclusion of the rebellion Tsêng was appointed Viceroy of the Liang kiang provinces, now divided into the three provinces of Kiangnan, Kiangsi, and Anhui. Under the imperial scheme of government the viceroys enjoyed a peculiar position. In fact, they were independent autocrats in their respective viceroyalties subject to recall whenever the central government in Peking disapproved of the way in which they were using the authority thus delegated to them. Many functions and responsibilities which in Occidental countries would fall logically to the central government in China were assumed by the viceroys. A viceroy in the coastal provinces, for instance, had his own department of foreign affairs through which he carried on relations with the foreigners in his viceroyalty quite independently of other viceroys and of the Imperial Government. The same was true of such innovations as the establishment of arsenals and dockyards equipped with modern machinery and directed by foreign engineers. The responsibility for such innovations

25

was left to the individual viceroy, subject only to the disapproval of the Court. This method of conducting affairs was very convenient for the Imperial Government as it could thus escape responsibility for any unpopular or unsuccessful innovation and, at the same time, it could check or encourage at will unusual departures from the ordinary routine. Prior to 1900 nearly all attempts to modernize the army and navy of China and to build telegraphs and railroads were undertaken by viceroys who were favorable toward westernization.

Tsêng had heard of Yung Wing through the famous mathematician and student of western science, Li Jen-shu. In 1863 Yung Wing was surprised to receive a request from Tsêng Kuo-fan to visit him at his headquarters in Anking. Somewhat disturbed by an invitation from a powerful official, Yung Wing found, much to his delight when he arrived at Anking, that Tsêng Kuo-fan wanted to talk to him about the things most dear to his heart—plans for the reformation of China. The upshot of this visit was that Tsêng commissioned Yung Wing to go to America to buy machinery to equip an arsenal and machine shop to be established at Shanghai. This arsenal was not only to manufacture arms and ammunition, but it was to construct steam vessels and to be a school for the training of young Chinese in the mechanical arts of the West.

Yung Wing had hoped to present to Tsêng his plan for sending Chinese youths abroad to be educated in the technical professions, but upon the advice of his friends who had been instrumental in getting him invited to Anking, Yung Wing temporarily shelved his radical educational proposal for the more practical one of establishing an arsenal. This was the opportunity for which he had long been looking. Tsêng was the most powerful official in the empire, and whatever he proposed to the Court would be sure to receive a favorable hearing. Yung Wing could afford to postpone his educational scheme, while he carried out the arsenal commission for Tsêng Kuo-fan.

He arrived in America in 1864, in the midst of the Civil War. Machine shops everywhere were working at full capacity turning out munitions and war machinery for the Federal Government. But he managed to get his order executed by the firm of Putnam and Company of Fitchburg, Massachusetts. While waiting for the machinery to be completed, Yung Wing visited his alma mater, renewing there many pleasant acquaintances of his college days. He then visited Washington for the purpose of offering himself as a six months' volunteer in the Union Army. He was brought to do this by a strong sense of duty, because in 1852 he had become an American citizen. His offer was not taken up, however, for the officers in charge of the Volunteer Department did not wish to interfere with his duties to the Chinese Government.

In 1865 upon the completion of the machinery, Yung Wing returned with it to China. A site near Shanghai had been procured for the new arsenal where extensive buildings had been constructed, ready for the installation of the new machinery. Thus was begun the great Kiangnan Arsenal which was to play such an important part in the westernization of China. Here guns and ammunition were manufactured and machinery for the fabrication of tools was set up. A school was attached to the arsenal in which there was trained a corps of mechanics. A translating department was organized in which a staff, under the capable direction of Dr. John Fryer, began the task of translating into Chinese the basic works of the various branches of science.

As a reward for the faithful execution of the task of purchasing the machinery for the arsenal, Tsêng Kuo-fan memorialized the throne recommending that Yung Wing be given a regular official rank. He was appointed to the fifth grade and made Expectant Taotai which in theory at least gave him the right to be appointed to a prefecture whenever a vacancy occurred. While awaiting appointment to a prefecture, he was given the position of interpreter and translator for the Chinese authorities at Shanghai. Tsêng did this not only to reward Yung Wing but to give him official standing, without which he could command little regard from the majority of Chinese officials. Yung Wing had at last found the influential official who recognized the value of his western education, and until the death of Tsêng in 1872 the two men worked together to introduce into China the scientific knowledge of the Occident.

Even such a powerful official as Tsêng Kuo-fan, however, had to proceed slowly with such an unusual proposal as to suggest that Chinese youths be sent abroad to be educated in the scientific professions. His arguments had to be couched in language acceptable to the conservative court circle. The humiliations which China had suffered in the wars of 1840 and 1856 had intensified the dislike of most of the mandarinate for Western civilization. At the same time, it had made the more discerning officials very conscious of the fact that China could never hope to check the aggressive tendencies of the West by any means other than by mastering the technology which enabled the West to be aggressive in its relations with China. The majority of the officials remained steadfast in their dislike of Occidental science and machinery.

Yung Wing fully realized that the military power of the Occidental nations rested on a much broader basis than the mere application of machine technology to the arts of war. He understood that it was the product of a whole way of life, a way of life decidedly antagonistic to the philosophic, balanced civilization of China. But Yung Wing seems not to have been disturbed by the evident fact that in the measure that China adopted the machinery of the West, the old traditional Chinese civilization would be undermined and eventually destroyed. He showed very little concern over this inevitable outcome. He was a typical product of western education, so much so that he was regarded in official circles as a foreigner rather than as a Chinese.

Tsêng's experiments in building China's first steam vessels at the arsenals at Anking and Kiangnan (Shanghai), gave him some comprehension of the network of highly developed technical skills required by modern armies and navies. In pursuit of his immediate aim of strengthening China's armed forces he was exceedingly desirous of introducing these technical skills into China as rapidly as possible. He hoped eventually to establish a series of training schools patterned after the training centers attached to the arsenals. These schools, however, depended upon a staff of foreign experts who had to be paid high salaries, and whose first loyalty was to their own nations rather than to China. Tsêng wanted to replace these foreign experts with professionally-trained Chinese. In the meantime, he determined to speed up the process of creating a body of Chinese engineers, by sending abroad a group of young Chinese to study map-making, coastal surveying, navigation, shipbuilding, the design and construction of machinery, and the manufacture of arms and ammunition.

There is little ground for thinking that Tsêng Kuo-fan had more in mind than the immediate aim of giving such youths technical training in these practical pursuits. On the other hand, Yung Wing had the much deeper conception of giving them a thorough western education. As the direction of the project finally fell into his hands, it was given this deeper and, in some respects, anti-Chinese direction. In pursuing his aims, Yung Wing brought upon the Educational Mission the criticism of the majority of Chinese officials, who remained steadfastly hostile to a project which, it seemed to them, not only cast reflection upon the traditional Confucian basis of Chinese education but also had the effect of so westernizing the students who went abroad that they returned to China alien in their outlook and habits.

Yung Wing's opportunity to get his Educational Mission scheme presented to the Throne arose at the time of the so-called

Tientsin massacre of 1870. In the autumn of that year, Tsêng Kuo-fan and Li Hung-chang were among the Imperial Commissioners sent to Tientsin to settle with the French authorities the difficulties arising out of a mob murder of several French subjects. Another of the Commissioners was Ting Jih-chang, Governor of Kiangsu, long a leading exponent of the adoption of western machinery by China. Yung Wing was appointed secretary to the Commissioners and after the Tientsin affair was settled he was invited by the Commissioners to prepare a detailed plan for sending groups of Chinese youths to the schools of Europe and America. The project was finally incorporated into a memorial which was presented to the throne by Tsêng Kuo-fan and Li Hung-chang.

In this memorial Tsêng and his colleagues first reviewed the disasters that had fallen upon China because of her inability to resist the aggressions of the Western nations. They then proceeded to lecture the Throne upon the necessity of acquiring the technical accomplishments of the West if China ever hoped to be free. The memorialists then proposed the daring plan of sending abroad a number of Chinese and Manchu youths to be educated in the professions intimately connected with the arts of war. Throughout this memorial, and in all the successive memorials having to do with the plan, the whole stress was placed upon the acquisition of the technical knowledge of the West, not as something desirable in itself nor as something likely to relieve the poverty of the Chinese masses, but solely as means whereby China would be enabled to resist foreign aggression. Tsêng Kuo-fan and Li Hung-chang, together with all the mandarin reformers of this period, seemed to think that the Occidental nations had discovered some magic formula which gave them their military and naval strength and that all that China needed was to discover this formula and use it against the foreigners as the foreigners were now using it against the Chinese.

It was in this spirit that they proposed to make a beginning by sending to the United States thirty youths a year for four years. The lads were to be between the ages of twelve and twenty and in their selection no distinction was to be made between Manchu and Chinese. Full consent of the parents or guardians had to be obtained to keep the youths abroad for a period of fifteen to twenty years. Moreover the students had to promise that they would not return of their own accord before the end of that time, nor would they upon returning engage in private enterprise. Upon their return to China, they were to receive a regular official rank and were to have all the prestige of the officials who had entered the imperial service by means of the Confucian examination system.

In order to overcome opposition from the conservatives at Court, it was proposed that Yung Wing should not have sole charge of the Educational Mission but that he should share its direction with Ch'en Lan-pin. The latter was only a minor official in the Board of Punishments, but he had a great reputation as a stickler for Confucian etiquette and he was well known for his devotion to Confucian learning. The fact that only a minor official was appointed co-director with Yung Wing shows how unimportant the Court considered the project.

The appointment of Ch'en Lan-pin proved to be unfortunate. He never had the remotest conception of the significance of the Educational Mission, and when he found himself transported to the unfamiliar and uncomfortable environment of America, his one concern was to get back to China as soon as he possibly could.

It was estimated that the total cost of the Mission would amount to about one million two-hundred thousand taels, truly an enormous sum for agricultural China to spend on what most of the mandarinate must have considered to be a hair-brained scheme of Tsêng Kuo-fan and Li Hung-chang. To overcome the difficulty of raising this amount and to insure the regular remit-tance of the funds necessary to support the Mission, provision was made to set aside from the receipts of the Imperial Maritime Customs at Shanghai specified annual sums.

In order to safeguard the students from being "enclosed by foreign learning" and to keep before them the Confucian ideal of loyalty to the Emperor, a staff of Chinese teachers was to accompany the Mission and instruct the students in the Chinese language and Confucian classics. Specific provision was made for periodic assemblies of the students to hear the Sacred Edict read to them and to enable them to make the proper ceremonial obeisances in the direction of the Emperor's residence in Peking.

In the memorials relating to the establishment of the Educational Mission it was proposed that the United States be the country in which this initial experiment was to be carried on. Later, similar contingents of students could be sent to Europe, but all of the one-hundred and twenty students embraced in the original project were to be sent to the United States. What were the reasons which led Tsêng Kuo-fan and Li Hung-chang to choose the United States rather than Great Britain, France or Germany? The Japanese, confronted with the same choice, chose Germany because they believed that Germany's success in the Franco-German war had established her as the foremost military power in Europe. Furthermore, the political organization of Germany was more suited to Japan's aristocratic society than were the democratic parliamentary systems of France and Great Britain. These considerations should have appealed also to the Chinese but the European countries were passed over in favor of the United States. The fact that Yung Wing had passed through the educational systems of America and therefore had a first hand knowledge of the problems that would confront the young Chinese in the American environment obviously was an important reason for choosing the United States. But the decisive reason was that in 1868 the United States had concluded a treaty with China on a strictly reciprocal basis. This treaty specifically provided for mutual rights of residence and attendance at the public schools by the citizens of the two countries. Tsêng Kuo-fan and Li Hung-chang were keenly appreciative of the mutually beneficial nature of the treaty of 1868, and the choice of the United States as the country for China's first adventure in western education was a marked way of showing this appreciation.

In the Spring of 1871, the Court gave its sanction to the scheme and commanded Tsêng Kuo-fan and Li Hung-chang to set up the organization of the Chinese Educational Mission. A Bureau was established at Shanghai with officials appointed to supervise the selection of candidates. A school was established where they could receive preliminary training and where their fitness for the long stay abroad could be ascertained. This school was opened in the Summer of 1871, but not before an unexpected obstacle to the success of the Mission had arisen. This was the somewhat embarrassing fact that in the Yangtze Valley and in the northern provinces practically no candidates responded to the invitation of the local magistrates to enter the school at Shanghai. In China, the land where gains come only from hard labor, the offer of the Government to educate the students and to pay them a modest stipend while they were abroad was received with the greatest suspicion. Moreover, the Chinese with their great sense of family ties were exceedingly reluctant to see their sons disappear into an unknown land of the West for a period so long that it practically amounted to permanent separation. The dearth of candidates caused Yung Wing to make a hurried tour through the Canton area where the prejudice against foreigners had been somewhat softened by long contact and where could be found many Chinese youths who had received some instruction in English in the mission schools. The result was that of the one-hundred and twenty lads who were finally sent to the United States, over 70 per cent of them were from the region around Canton. In fact, thirty-seven of the total were from Yung Wing's own district of Hsiang Shan. In the third and fourth contingents there was a larger proportion of students from the North. By 1873 and 1874 the project was beginning to prove itself, with the result that the sons of wealthier and more prominent families now sought places in the Mission. It is noteworthy that not a single Manchu ever volunteered to exile himself among the "western barbarians" in order to serve better the country which his ancestors had conquered.

Yung Wing preceded the first students to America to make arrangements for their arrival. This group, comprising thirty students, the Co-Commissioner, Ch'en Lan-pin, and a staff of Chinese teachers and interpreters, sailed from Shanghai in the summer of 1872. When Yung Wing arrived in New Haven, he called on President Porter of Yale College to seek advice as to the best way to proceed with the students' education. Most of them spoke little English and, of course, were totally unfamiliar with the American environment. President Porter strongly advised Yung Wing not to keep the young Chinese lads together in one group but to place them by twos and threes in American families. Furthermore, President Porter suggested that the boys would learn to speak English more rapidly if they were scattered in the villages and towns of the Connecticut Valley. Yung Wing heartily agreed with this plan, and with the cooperation of the faculty of Yale College and the Connecticut State Board of Education, he made the necessary arrangements to put this plan in operation. People readily volunteered to take the young Chinese boys into their homes, so that when they finally arrived in Hartford more than enough homes had been found in which to place them. These families were amply paid for their services by the Educational Mission, but the immediate response to the calls for homes and the quality of the families who opened their homes to the boys demonstrated that there was a genuine desire on the part of the people of Connecticut to share in an experiment which held such promise for the future of China. Nearly always the local minister, the local school teacher, and the local doctor each took two or three of the boys into his family.

Within a few days after their arrival at Hartford, the students found themselves sharing the daily life of the particular family to which they had been assigned and living in typical New England villages. It was a rather Spartan-like way to proceed with the education of these young Chinese lads, but it certainly introduced them thoroughly to their American environment in the shortest possible time. They became Americanized with bewildering rapidity. In no time they learned the language of the schoolroom and the playground. They soon shed their long silk gowns and with them their dignified Chinese manners. Within a few months they were on the best of terms with their American schoolmates and were competing for honors both in their classes and on the baseball diamond. In their American homes they were taught western table manners and were introduced to the somewhat severe discipline of New England family life. Y. T. Woo, one of the boys who lived in the Bartlett home in Hartford, recalls some of his early experiences. He writes, "I remember Miss Mary Bartlett was a strict disciplinarian. When we held our knives and forks too low at meals, she would correct us. When she heard us talking in our rooms in the attic after nine or ten p.m., she would call from below, 'Boys, stop talking, it is time to sleep.' Old Mr. Bartlett used to have Prayer Meetings mornings and evenings each day."

So completely did the boys succumb to the American environment that, in time, it became increasingly difficult to keep them at their Chinese studies. Yung Wing favored this complete break with Chinese habits and he was not much concerned about their neglect of their Chinese education. His attitude opened the conduct of the Mission to severe criticism by those in China unfavorably disposed towards it, and in the long run it was one of the chief reasons why the Mission was prematurely abandoned.

CHAPTER III

CHINA'S FIRST HUNDRED: THE STUDENTS IN THE UNITED STATES

With what feelings of mingled excitement and apprehension must the thirty young Chinese boys forming the first contingent of the Educational Mission have said goodbye to their parents and prepared to leave their homeland for a fifteen year stay in a strange and unknown country. America was a land so distant and so strange that they could not conjure up in their minds visions of what it might be like. The stories they had heard about it must have caused them to liken it to some fearful Taoist Hell. W. W. Yen, one of modern China's most distinguished returned students, relates how such stories caused him to miss the opportunity to become a student in the Educational Mission. When he was a lad, an official came to his village seeking families who would consent to have their sons sent abroad to be educated "at the expense of the government". His parents were greatly attracted by this unusual offer and thought of consenting to his going, but they drew back when the local wiseacres frightened the boys of the village by telling them that "the wild men over there would skin us alive, graft the skins of dogs onto our bodies and exhibit us as they would some uncommon animal."

Stories such as these kept most parents from taking advantage of the opportunity to have their sons educated at no expense to themselves. The boys who made up the first contingent came from families who either were accustomed to foreigners by being in daily contact with them at Canton or Shanghai or had friends and relatives who had some first hand knowledge of the foreigners and who persuaded the reluctant parents to let their sons go.

Yen Fu-lee, who came over with the second contingent in 1873, describes how his widowed mother was induced by one

36

of his cousins to permit him to volunteer. This cousin was in the tea business in Shanghai and he "came home with glowing accounts of the new movement; and so painted the golden prospects of the successful candidates that he persuaded my mother to let me go."

In preparation for their long stay abroad the students were provided with outfits of the traditional long gowns of the Chinese scholar and with other articles of clothing which would enable them to present a dignified appearance when they arrived in the United States. After paying their respects to the Taotai, or Chief Magistrate of Shanghai, and calling upon the American Consul, they then, as one of the students wrote, "with heavy hearts and vague feelings of the future, waved farewell to their weeping relatives and smiling friends on shore."

From Shanghai the first detachment went to Yokohama where they were transferred to the paddle-wheel steamer "China" bound for San Francisco. A three day stay in San Francisco introduced them to the amenities of American civilization and no doubt caused them to lose some of their apprehension as to what was to be their fate. Their journey across the United States was an exciting experience. Passing through the prairie country, they saw, as one of the lads wrote, "genuine red Indians with eagle feathers projecting from their black hair, their faces painted in different colours, similar to the painted actors on the Chinese stage, and armed with bows and arrows."

Upon their arrival in Hartford, Connecticut, they were met by Yung Wing who assigned them to the various families who were to take the Chinese boys into their homes. Within a few days they were scattered in a score of little towns throughout of the Connecticut Valley. Yen Fu-lee, who later became an editor of a Chinese paper in New York, says in his reminiscences, "It was my good fortune to be placed into the hands of a most motherly lady in Springfield. She came after us in a hack. As I was pointed out to her, she put her arms around me and kissed me. This made the rest of the boys laugh, and perhaps I got rather red in the face; however, I would say nothing to show my embarrassment. But that was the first kiss I ever had had since my infancy." As he and the other lad who had been placed in the care of this lady spoke only a little English, the first weeks were ones of many adjustments. The boys were dressed in their Chinese dress: long satin gown, cue and silk shoes. On the first Sunday in their new home they were told to get ready to attend Sunday school, but, only catching the word "school" and thinking that they were now to embark upon their educational careers, they wrapped up their books and prepared to meet the ordeal which they had been anticipating for many months. To their consternation they found themselves entering a Church. As the students had been warned against the attempts which would be made to Christianize them, the two boys immediately rushed from the Church and back to the safety of their rooms. Eventually, however, several of the boys were converted to Christianity, but most of them stayed obdurate in the face of the steady pressure of their hosts to bring them into the fold.

The Americanization of these young Chinese lads went on with remarkable speed. With few exceptions they were between the ages of twelve and sixteen and were no different from the young people of any other land in being very sensitive to anything that might reflect upon their personal appearance or make them markedly different from the majority of the youths around them. At first they were required to wear their long Chinese gowns and plaited cues. It made them look like girls and their fellow American students took great delight in teasing them and calling them Chinese girls. These taunts led to many blows and black eyes and a determination on the part of the Chinese lads to abandon their Chinese dresses for American trousers and coats. This caused one of the first clashes between Yung Wing and his colleague, Ch'en Lan-pin. Yung Wing sympathized with the predicament of the lads, but Ch'en was shocked by their determination to forsake the long gown, the traditional badge of the Chinese scholar.

Much as they wished to do so, the boys were not allowed to cut off their cues, as the cue was the emblem of obedience and loyalty to the Manchu regime. In the end some of the lads became so imbued with the free spirit of their environment that they did cut off their cues. In such instances, the offender was promptly sent back to China.

Mrs. Annie Smith of Lee, Massachusetts, recalling her girlhood days, says of the two Chinese boys who were sent to her village to attend school: "They were with Deacon Alexander Hyde, and their first appearance with him at church made quite a sensation in our quiet village; their garments were of beautiful stiff brocaded satin; thick soled and padded slippers and round satin caps. One of their first escapades was the wild chasing of a neighbour's pigs through the village and down to the 'Flats'. It was not long before they appeared at school in American clothes of dark blue flannel, with queus neatly braided around their heads or concealed down the back under their coats."

During his stay in Lee, one of the boys became greatly interested in raising and breeding chickens. He kept a flock of the Plymouth Rock breed in the yard of Deacon Hyde's home, and when, in 1881, the students were suddenly ordered to return to China, he took home with him a crate of these chickens.

Miss Louise Bartlett, the daughter of Mrs. Fannie Bartlett, in whose home lived several of the Mission Students during many years of their stay in the United States, recalls her impressions of these Chinese boys. She says: "They were very youthful as I looked upon them as playmates, very bright and full of fun, generally winning in games as soon as we taught them to them and picking up English so fast that I do not remember except at the very first any difficulty in communicating with them. They were soon favorites with their schoolmates and de-

39

lighted their teachers by their progress after they began to attend a public school."

The Bartlett family had remarkably close connections with the first reaching out towards America of such Chinese pioneers as Yung Wing. Mrs. Fannie Bartlett was the widow of Professor David Bartlett, of the New York School for the Blind. The Bartletts had been the first ones to greet Yung Wing and his companions when the Reverend Samuel Robbins Brown had brought them to America in 1847. It will be recalled that the Reverend Mr. Brown went out to China to take charge of the school of the Morrison Educational Society. Later he was invited by the Japanese Government to establish a school along Western lines in Tokyo. He thus had the remarkable distinction of being the founder of Western education in both China and Japan. He was related to the Bartlett family by marriage, as his wife was Elizabeth Bartlett, the niece of Professor David Bartlett.

In Hartford, Mrs. Fannie Bartlett and her three daughters, May, Margaret, and Louise, became the devoted friends and counsellors of the Chinese boys who came into their family. In later life in China, the boys who stayed in the Bartlett household always remembered with great appreciation and affection the years they spent in this quiet home in Hartford, Connecticut. In 1910, Miss Louise and Miss Mary Bartlett were invited by Liang Tun-yen, one of their former charges, to spend a whole year in China. These two delightful New England ladies accepted the invitation and for one year they lived like Chinese princesses amidst the luxurious surroundings of the family of a wealthy Chinese official.

In 1874 the Chinese Government authorized Yung Wing to erect a headquarters building for the Educational Mission in Hartford, Connecticut. Yung Wing urged this move as he believed that the establishment of a permanent headquarters owned by the Chinese Government would assure the continuation of the Mission. He wanted the Educational Mission "as deeply rooted in the United States as possible, so as not to give the Chinese Government any chance of retrograding in this movement." The building, which cost $75,000, served not only as a general headquarters but also as a residence for the students during those periods when they were called in from the outlying towns to the Hartford headquarters to receive instruction in the Chinese language and Confucian classics.

In 1874, Ch'en Lan-pin, the Co-Commissioner, was recalled to China and his place was taken by Ngen Yoh-liang. The relationship between Yung Wing and Ch'en Lan-pin had not been very harmonious. Ch'en remained untouched by his sojourn in America and looked with great disfavor upon the rapid and thorough Americanization of the students of the Mission. His reports to the Imperial Government were not very favorable, but as long as Li Hung-chang stood back of the Mission it was fairly safe. Li was an adept politician, however, and changed his enthusiasm as political discretion dictated. At this time, 1874, the relations between the United States and China were still very cordial. The reciprocal nature of the Sino-American treaty of July 28, 1868, had not yet been modified by Congress nor had the influx of Chinese labourers into the western United States been magnified into a national issue by political agitation. Later, this era of good feelings was to give way to one of racial discrimination against the Chinese in the United States and of keen disappointment at the Court in Peking because of the discriminatory legislation passed by the American Congress.

In 1875 there occurred an event which greatly furthered the suspicion with which many of the conservative Chinese statesmen viewed Yung Wing and his ardent championing of "westernization". He, very frankly, desired to saturate the Chinese students with an American viewpoint and in consequence he neglected their Chinese education, which according to the original plan was to parallel their Occidental training. He had also been converted to Christianity, and in 1852 he had become an American citizen. He now took the further step of marrying an American woman, Miss Louise Kellogg, the daughter of one of Hartford's leading physicians. The ceremony was performed by the Reverend J. H. Twichell of Hartford, and in his diary he has left an interesting account of the marriage. Under the date of February 24, 1875, he notes:

"Married my beloved friend Mandarin Yung Wing of the Chinese Educational Mission to Miss Mary L. Kellogg, of Avon, Connecticut. The engagement was entered into about a year ago. Miss K. was teacher (at her home) of two of the pupils of the Mission. The match was a good deal commented on. Some people feel doubtfully about it; some disapprove of it utterly; some (like me) gloried in it. I have felt from the outset that in case it should not injure Wing in China or hamper him in his life work in any way, it was to be altogether rejoiced in. My wife and I often used (before this union was contemplated) to suggest the thought of marriage to Wing as we sat at our fireside, and to his reply that there was no Chinese woman whom he would marry and no American lady who would marry him, we have many a time replied that as for the latter point he had no proof of it, and that we didn't believe he judged rightly upon it. Possibly we helped him to venture in the matter. I shall await the result of the step with great interest, and with confidence that only good will come of it. I drove over with Wing and Dr. Kellogg in a carriage and made a very difficult passage of the mountain owing to the ice. I returned by carriage also with Yeh Shu Tung and Yung Yen Foo [Chinese teachers attached to the Mission]. The presence of these Chinese gentlemen in their strange dress at a solemn religious service and social festival in a Puritan home in a Connecticut country town was a striking, and to me, excedingly impressive feature of the occasion. After the marriage and tetotal feast, Wing, Kellogg, Mrs. Bartlett, and I retired to a room that had formerly been

42

the study of the ancestral ministerial Kellogg, and there for form's sake and to do the affair on hand justice in their eyes, took a glass of wine with Messers. Yeh and Yung."

Yung Wing's marriage proved to be personally very happy for himself and his wife, but it undoubtedly deepened the opposition to the Mission among the many conservative officials in Peking who persisted in looking upon the Mission as a stain upon the honor of Confucian China. By this marriage Yung Wing had two sons, Morrison Brown Yung and Bartlett Golden Yung. Unfortunately, Yung Wing's wife died in June, 1886. This event, coming after the dashing of all his hopes and plans by the recall of the Educational Mission in 1881, left Yung Wing a lonely man. His two sons were his chief joy during the rest of his life. They were both educated at Yale University. Eventually they settled in China and married Chinese wives. Morrison Brown Yung died in Peking in 1934. Bartlett Golden Yung still lives with his family in Shanghai, where he is an engineer of some note.

In the autumn of 1875, Yung Wing received word from the Chinese Government that he and Ch'en Lan-pin, the former Co-Commissioner of the Educational Mission, had been appointed joint Ministers to the United States. This was a signal honor, but one which Yung Wing did not want His greatest desire was to be left in active direction of the Mission, and he begged Li Hung-chang to intercede with the Imperial Government to permit him to continue his work at Hartford. His request was met, in part at least, by making him Associate Minister at Washington, with Ch'en Lan-pin as Chief Minister. At the same time, Yung Wing was permitted to remain in general charge of the Mission, although his new diplomatic duties caused him to spend much time away from Hartford.

When, in 1878, Ch'en Lan-pin returned from China to assume his post at Washington as the first Chinese Minister to the United States, he brought with him a new Commissioner who, under Yung Wing's supervision, was to have charge of the Educational Mission. The new commissioner was Woo Tzê-têng. The exact motive back of his appointment is difficult to determine, but, judging by his actions, he probably was sent by foes of the Mission in order to discredit it. From the beginning of his arrival at Hartford, he sent back to Peking a stream of unfavorable reports on the management of the Mission and upon the un-Chinese conduct of the students. He might have been sent by Li Hung-chang, who, now that the Mission was being very unfavorably talked about in China, no longer found it politically expedient to support it and sought a means to bring it to an end. In any case, with the arrival of this individual, the recall of the Mission was only a question of time. He and Yung Wing clashed from the beginning of his term as Commissioner. Woo Tzê-têng was profoundly shocked at the care-free manners which the Chinese students had adopted. He felt that they had lost all of the qualities associated with the Confucian scholars who composed the official class in China. Their Chinese studies had been neglected to the point where some of the students were actually forgetting their own language. They knew very little and expressed hardly any desire to know more about the Chinese classics, which in China formed the basis of all education. Even if they had wished to do so, the Chinese youths could not have resisted the overwhelming pressures of the American environment. After several years in America they acted, talked and thought like typical American boys. Their pocket money allowance of one dollar per month in no way satisfied the many wants that their surroundings stimulated. Several got into debt and were sent home. The fact that some of them cut off their cues or became Christians was regarded as particularly alarming evidence of their separation from Chinese culture. Yung Wing welcomed the metamorphis taking place in the students, but such typical Chinese officials as Ch'en Lan-pin and Woo Tzê-têng hardly could be expected to look with

44

complacency upon such a complete westernization of the students as was taking place.

A case in point was that of Yung Kwai, a nephew of Yung Wing. When it was learned that he had become a Christian, he was deprived of his place in the Mission just as he was ready to enter Harvard College. Moreover, he committed the grave offense of cutting off his cue, which would have brought upon him severe punishment once he returned to China. Fortunately, at this juncture, the Reverend J. H. Twichell, ever a friend of the boys of the Mission while they were in Hartford, intervened to help Yung Kwai out of his difficulties. In his diary under the date of December, 1880, he records how Dr. Yung Wing secretly provided the necessary funds for Yung Kwai to stay in America and to finish his education. He writes:

> "Yung Kwai was after all, when he had graduated at the Springfield High School, and had passed his examinations to enter Harvard College, deprived of his place in the Educational Mission, and ordered to return to China, together with several other of the students, some of whom had behaved badly and some whose health forbade them to continue their studies. One other besides Yung Kwai had offended by his religious course.
>
> "Dr. Yung Wing came to me and offered to pay Yung Kwai's college expenses, at the rate of $700 a year, if he could manage to stay in the country, the only considerations being, first that he would repay the money when he could, and second that he would tender his services to the Chinese Government when his education was completed. Desiring to conceal his connection with the matter, Yung Wing directed me to instruct or request Yung Kwai to inform him as a piece of news of this offer and ask his opinion as to accepting it. Accordingly on my way

45

to Keene Valley in August, Yung Kwai met me by appointment at Springfield and I opened the business to him. The result was that when some weeks later the company of students returning to China set out, Yung Kwai and the other offender in religion, Tan Yew-fun, whose fellow students of his own detachment had meanwhile offered to contribute enough from their allowances to pay his way through Yale College, slipped away from the rest at Springfield, went into concealment, and remained behind."

Tan Yew-fun entered Yale College and was graduated with the class of 1883. His career was soon cut short, however, as within a few months of graduation he contracted pneumonia and died. He was buried in the village cemetery of Colbrook, Connecticut, where his grave is still marked by a stone bearing a Chinese inscription. Such instances as the conversion to Christianity of Yung Kwai and Tan Yew-fun were reported back to China in their most unfavorable light by Woo Tzê-têng, causing the Mission to be viewed with grave concern by the Chinese mandarinate and by the Court.

Furthermore, the relations between the United States and China now began to lose their former amicable character. The Mission had been inaugurated in a glow of friendly feeling brought about by the reciprocal nature of the Burlingame treaty of 1868. Anson Burlingame, who served as the United States Minister to the Imperial Chinese Government between 1861 and 1867, not only introduced a policy of friendly cooperation between China and the United States but he succeeded in no small measure in inducing the whole diplomatic corps in Peking to give up its traditional gunboat policy of threats for·one of cooperation towards the Imperial Government. His enthusiasm for establishing the relations of China with the United States and the European powers upon a friendly and reciprocal basis was so great that in 1867 he resigned his post as American Minister to become the representative of the Chinese Government upon a diplomatic mission to the United States and Europe. The Sino-American treaty of 1868 was the most promising result of his efforts in this direction.

The American Government, however, showed little disposition actually to treat the Chinese in the United States upon a basis of equality. The so-called Chinese question arose in the western states and was seized upon by politicians as a means of riding into office upon an ever swelling wave of racial discrimination. Riots directed against the Chinese occurred, notably in Denver and Wyoming, but the American Government did nothing to secure the safety of the Chinese or pay compensation for loss of life or damage done to Chinese-owned property. When Yung Wing and Ch'en Lan-pin, in their capacities as Ministers at Washington, complained that such actions against Chinese citizens were violations of the Burlingame Treaty, the American Government replied that states' rights gave it no power to interfere. Finally, with little regard for the dignity of the Chinese Government, the reciprocal provisions of the Burlingame treaty were arbitrarily abrogated by a race-conscious Congress. Thereafter, Chinese immigrants were excluded from entering the United States.

All these high-handed proceedings offended the Chinese Court and spoiled the good impression made by the Burlingame treaty. Moreover, these events played into the hands of a conservative group of officials in Peking who were striving to wrest control of the Imperial Government from the hands of more liberal statesmen, such as Li Hung-chang and Tso Tsung-t'ang. Li, himself, had been severely disappointed in his hopes that when the students of the Educational Mission were ready, as they now were, many of them would be permitted to pass through the United States military and naval academies at West Point and Annapolis. When Li made inquiries through the American Minister in Peking as to the possibility of the Chinese students entering these government institutions, he was greatly taken aback when he was informed that it required a special act of Congress for foreigners to enter either academy and that there was little likelihood of Congress passing such special legislation. Yet the Burlingame Treaty specifically provided for the reciprocal right of American and Chinese students to enter the government schools of either nation. Once Li Hung-chang found that the students from the Educational Mission would not be able to obtain military and naval training at West Point or Annapolis, he favored sending Chinese students to England, Germany, and France, where they were readily welcomed in the government military and naval academies.

In the face of the above circumstances, it became increasingly impolitic for Li Hung-chang to defend the Mission against the attacks of the conservative group at Court. Li also seemed to have lost interest in sending any great numbers of students abroad. By this time several arsenals and dockyards had been established in China with training schools attached to them in which students could receive technical instruction. It was true that such institutions made it necessary to employ at great expense foreign experts but, on the other hand, such institutions had nominal Chinese heads and a staff of Chinese teachers and employees. In this way, the political necessity of providing jobs for the job hungry people was in some measure satisfied. Moreover, there is ample reason to believe that one of the real reasons for the severe criticism of Yung Wing's management of the Mission was that he kept its financial affairs in his own hands and did not permit the customary peculations associated with a Chinese government enterprise.

By 1881 Li Hung-chang was ready to withdraw his support from the Mission. In a long letter, dated March 30, 1881, to the Tsung Li Yamen (Foreign Office), Li discussed the question whether or not the Mission should be withdrawn. He admitted that the majority of the students had been sent abroad at such an early age that it was unavoidable that they should become corrupted by Western customs. He said that he continually warned Yung Wing not to neglect the Chinese education of the students but his warnings had little results. Li agreed that to terminate the Mission abruptly might leave a bad impression in America, particularly in view of the fact that ex-President Grant, on his visit to China, had specifically requested that the boys be permitted to continue their studies. Finally, Li said that the expenses of the Mission were very great and that the continuous flow of funds from China for its support was not good for the Imperial Government. He left the final decision to the Tsung Li Yamen, but it is evident from the whole tenor of his letter that he was no longer willing to champion the Mission. Without his positive support, it was doomed. In consequence, on June 8, 1881, the Tsung Li Yamen ordered that the Educational Mission be abolished and that the teachers and students return to China as soon as possible.

The verdict of the Imperial Government was received with deep disappointment by the Chinese students in America. This disappointment was shared by many Americans who had come in contact with the students during their ten year stay in the United States. An attempt was made to induce the Chinese Government to rescind its order of recall but to no avail. The Reverend Joseph Twichell notes in his diary the events leading to the recall of the Mission and the efforts he made to avert the recall. He writes:

> During the month of October [1880], Yung Wing, in consequence of new perils having arisen, threatening the existence of the Mission, chiefly through the alarming representations made to the Chinese Government by Wu [Tzê-têng], the Commissioner, asked me to draw up a circular, to be signed by the heads of all the higher class of institutions at which the students had been placed, expressing the opinion that the

49

scheme of the Mission was excellent, its success so far manifest, and that its abandonment was greatly to be deplored. This I did, and forwarded the circular to U. S. Minister Angell, with the request that he present it to the viceroy, Li Hung-chang . . . .

Wing wrote to me asking me to go to New York and see Gen. Grant, and try to enlist his services on behalf of the Mission, the prospect of which was by this time darker still . . . I went to my friend Mark Twain and solicited his good offices in aiding me to gain access to Gen. G. with whom he had an acquaintance. He readily undertook to do this and wrote to Gen. Grant asking for both of us an interview with him the following Tuesday at New York. He also described to him the nature of the errand we were coming on and enclosed to him a copy of my lecture on the Mission. Dec. 21st, we were at the Fifth Ave. Hotel betimes in the morning, were received most kindly by Gen. Grant, who launched out in as free and flowing a talk as I ever heard, marked by broad, intelligent and benevolent views, on the subject of China, her wants, disadvantages. Now and then he asked a question, but kept the lead of the conversation. At last, he proposed of his own accord to write a letter to Li Hung Chang, advising the continuance of the Mission, asking only that I would prepare him some notes, giving him points to go by. Thus we succeeded easily beyond our expectation, thanks largely to Clemen's [Mark Twain] assistance.

The intervention of General Grant, brought about through the assistance of Mark Twain, proved effective in postponing, temporarily, the recall of the Mission. On March 10, 1881, Yung Wing informed the Reverend Mr. Twichell that he had received instructions from Li Hung-chang to continue the Mission, at least for the present. Yung Wing was greatly encouraged by the apparent change in policy of the Chinese Government, particularly as Li Hung-chang advised him that the Imperial Government was about to embark upon an extensive program of railroad building and that the United States would be called upon to furnish capital, men, and supplies for the projected railroads. But this period of enthusiasm gave way to one of profound disappointment. For it soon became evident that the Imperial Government had definitely decided to terminate the Mission and to recall the students and teachers. We are again indebted to the Reverend Mr. Twichell's diary for the story of these new developments. Under date of July 7, 1881, he notes:

> Yung Wing called to say that the new alarming dispatches from China of which I had heard, and which I had written him a note about, were in his opinion not what they seemed, so conflicting were they with the tenor of a letter just received from the Foreign Office in Peking. They seemed to seal the fate of the Mission, and when he told me what they were I doubted if his hope of a lighter meaning was justifiable.
>
> July 9th. Another dispatch from China received yesterday removes all doubt. The Mission is doomed. After all that has been done to save it, it must die ultimately and all its glorious promise fail. Alas. Alas. The disappointment of all its friends is extreme. Poor Wing, it is heaviest of all upon him. God sustain him. It is apparently, or in my judgment, the result of his separation from it. That gave the opposition a chance which has been abundantly improved. Surely 'tis a strange Providence.

This time, the Imperial Government was not to be swerved from its decision by the protests of the American supporters of the Mission. The Mission was at the mercy of political currents in Peking, and by the summer of 1881 those currents had turned against it. In July, 1881, the final orders were received to abandon the Mission and for all the teachers and students to return to China. The recall came at a particularly disastrous time for the students. Over sixty of them were then in colleges and technical schools, but the majority of these had just started their technical training in these schools. Another five years would have qualified them to be of great usefulness in engineering, mining, shipbuilding, communications and the various other branches of the technical professions. The great majority of the one hundred or so Chinese youths who returned to China in 1881 did prove themselves eventually in these fields, but only after years of discouragement and always under the handicap of insufficient training. Nevertheless, they infused a new spirit into the stagnant official atmosphere of old China. Their careers, with few exceptions spent in life-long service to the Chinese Government, radiated an energy and purpose conspicuously in contrast to the bureaucratic somnolence of the majority of officials by whom they were surrounded. Gradually, because of their real ability to get things done, the students of the Educational Mission came to the fore in Chinese public life. Many of them had very distinguished careers, and nearly all rendered great service to the new China that was emerging from the old.

CHAPTER IV

UNHAPPY LANDING: THE RETURN TO CHINA

Once the final order had been received from Peking to terminate the Educational Mission, it did not take the students and their teachers long to prepare for the journey back to China. They left Hartford, Connecticut, in July, 1881. In San Francisco they had to wait several days for the steamer which was to take them home. While waiting, they were challenged to a game by the Oakland baseball team. Won Bing-chung, who was destined to become one of China's foremost engineers, has left an amusing account of the game. He relates that "The Chinese nine had a twirler that played for Yale, and could do some wonderful curves with the ball, although in those days it was underhand pitching. Before the game began, the Oakland men imagined they were going to have a walk-over with the Chinese. Who had seen Celestials playing baseball fifty years ago? But the Oakland nine got the shock of their lives as soon as they attempted to connect with the deliveries of the Chinese pitcher; the fans were equally surprised at the strange phenomenon—Chinese playing their national ball game and showing the Yankees some of the thrills in the game. Unimaginable! All the same, the Chinese walloped them, to the great rejoicing of their comrades and fellow countrymen."

The pitcher whose unorthodox but entirely satisfactory delivery did so much to win the game against the Oakland team was Liang Tun-yen, who later rose to the highest positions in the Chinese Government. He was Minister of Foreign Affairs during the critical period just prior to the revolution of 1911, and after the revolution, he became Minister of Communications in the first Republican Government.

With this baseball victory to give a pleasant taste to their parting, the students embarked at San Francisco, bound for

Shanghai via Japan. Of the original one hundred and twenty who had been sent to the United States, about one hundred returned to China in August, 1882. Of the others, three had died in the United States, some had either been sent home for insubordination, or for getting into debt, or for cutting off their cues, while several refused to return and remained in America.

Let us try to visualize this group of young Chinese, for the most part just verging on manhood, as in the summer of 1881 they once again gazed upon their homeland from the rail of their slow moving ship. Before them lay Shanghai, not particularly changed in appearance from the last glimpse they had had of it some ten years before. Its harbor was as crowded as ever by numerous foreign steamers anchored in a long line in the center of the river. Everywhere there darted in and out of these steamers innumerable native craft. On shore a glimpse could be caught of the tall buildings on the Bund, along which flowed in never ending procession a stream of coolies engaged in the work of the port. But although Shanghai might remain substantially the same, this band of young Chinese was a vastly different group of individuals from the shy, apprehensive, long-gowned students who had started on their journey to America from this same city ten years earlier. Ten years in America, living in American homes, going to American public schools, studying American lessons under the direction of American teachers and constantly mixing with American lads of their own age, had left an indelible stamp upon them. Their habits, tastes, and outlook on life had become American. They thought, walked, and talked like Americans. Out of long usage they habitually spoke and referred to each other by the nicknames they had acquired. One was known as Breezy Jack, another as Sitting Bull, a third as Yankee Kwong. One lad had earned the sobriquet of Gorilla; another was spoken of as Buffalo Bill. Other choice names were Ajax, Alligator, Lady of the Lake, Cabbage, Irish King, Nigger Jew, Stork, Big Nose, Africanus, Spotted Tail, Dark Horse, Turkey, Nannigoat, and Country Cousin. These names are eloquent evidence of how deep the process of Americanization had gone in these Chinese lads. Among themselves they kept these schoolboy nicknames all through their lives, preserving them as if they were badges of distinction which marked them off from the masses of humanity around them.

Although their speech might be English, their faces betrayed the fact that they were returning to the home of their ancestors. What fate awaited these transformed and alien young Chinese in a land which still ringed youth with the iron customs of precedent and obedience to one's elders? Whatever awaited them, they had one bond to buoy up their hopes and that was the deep conviction that theirs was to be the task of leading China out of the morass of an effete Confucianism onto the firm ground of Western science and technology. They eagerly looked forward to this task, no doubt conjuring in their minds visions of brilliant careers and high honors showered upon them by a grateful nation. Rude indeed, then, must have been the shock of the indifferent and almost hostile reception that met them when they once stepped on shore. Wong Kai-kah, who later served with distinction in China's newly formed diplomatic service, has left a vivid description of this moment of homecoming. Writing to Mrs. Fannie Bartlett, in whose home at Hartford he had lived for several years, he describes these first few days thus:

Shanghai, China.
January 28, 1882

My dear Mrs. Bartlett,

You will be astonished to learn the shabby treatment we received at the hands of our paternal government. Perhaps you are already informed through some other source, but at any rate I will recount to you everything that has been done for our good (?)

The first sight of Shanghai as we steamed up to the warf thrilled us thinking what joyous welcome was waiting for us, and what a sea of familiar faces would soon surround us, and our country would soon extend her arms to embrace us in maternal kindness! But alas! Vain thoughts! Tall spires grew taller, the indistinct buildings grew more distinct, and we grew wilder and more enthusiastic over our imaginary reception, while the launch glided over the placid and yellow waters of the Yang Tze until it touched the wharf, with a sudden jar, which awoke us from our Utopian dreams. True a sea of faces was looking down on us, but no friendly recognition, no kindly smile greeted our forlorn band. Crowds of coolies, wheel-barrow, and jinrickshaw men were shouting, gesticulating and quarreling for business. One solitary man came aboard to receive us—our postal manager, Mr. Luk. Instead of employing carriages or boats to convey us to our destination, the Chinese Harbor Master's office, he packed us on wheel-barrows which have but one wheel and progress very slowly. And thus we were exposed to the gaping, jeering crowd who followed us. . . . Some of the wheelbarrows had no pass to go through the French concession, and many of us had to get down and walk, carrying our bags in our hands, an almost inexcusable act of debasing oneself in the eyes of the so-called Chinese gentleman.

We came to the Harbour Master's house, and after roll-call and a substantial supper, not elaborately prepared, we were dispatched with a detachment of Chinese marines acting as a guard over us to prevent our escaping from the grasp of our paternal government (?) to the "Knowledge Wishing Institution" inside the city behind the court of the Shanghai Taotai. Your

Western imagination is too sublime to conceive a place so vile as this so-called institution; you may have read about Turkish prisons or Andersonville Horrors, but compared with this they must have been enviable places.

But sleep, like death puts an end to all the evils and griefs and while the body is in the blessed arms of Morpheus extreme suffering of the present often leads our mind to the happy times of the past and to mingle over again with joy and mirth of bygone days. Grey morning and chilly wind brought us from our happy wanderings to stern reality again and the day wore away in vain hope of getting release from our confinement. It was doubly unfortunate for us in being shut up just at the time when the feast of the moon took place. There were many of us whose fathers, relatives and friends were awaiting us with wines and banquets in full preparation and longed to gaze upon and sit by the sides of their dear ones who had been so long away on the other hemisphere across the big sea. But such pleasures were denied them as we were to receive no liberty until we had made our "Kewtous" to the Shanghai Taotai. Accordingly, after four day's groaning and complaining, we were summoned to hold audience with the highest official in Shanghai. In three bodies we were mustered with enough guards to keep a regiment in quiet subjection; we commenced our journey amidst crowds of spectators whose comments were far from being flattering, and marched through piles of dirt and filth which commanded the entrance of the Taotai Yamen.

After much waiting and unnecessary delay we were at last ushered in to the presence of his Excellency and we prostrated ourselves before

57

his majestic presence; he however returned our
salute and motioned us to stand out each according to his division in which he went to America.
After he inquired of us our different accomplishments and the courses we pursued, the
"great Man" dismissed us allowing us to depart
from the "Prison" at 10 a.m. and returning at
4 p.m., much to the dislike of the boys. Two
days after, I boarded the English mail steamer
"Rosetta" and accompanied Yung Wei-chun to
Hongkong.

After a few days stay in Hongkong, Wong Kai-kah proceeded to Swatow, where his father had obtained the post of
Linguist in the Maritime Customs. When Wong arrived at
Swatow, he found, much to his embarrassment, that he could
not make the Swatow natives understand his Chinese, for they
spoke their own peculiar dialect. He therefore had to call upon
the aid of a passing English merchant to make the servants at
the Customs House understand what he wanted. After experi-
encing this curious episode of having a foreigner act as interpreter for him to his own countrymen, he was guided to his
father's house. But here again, the servants did not recognize
him and could not understand him. Finally, however, he was
admitted and was reunited with his family.

At the end of a short visit, he returned to Shanghai to
await the disposition of the Government. In Shanghai, he found
that many of his former schoolmates had already been sent to
the naval and telegraph schools at Tientsin, while a few were
attached to the yamens or offices of various governors and
magistrates. Writing again to Mrs. Bartlett, he says:

Alas! Friends whom I had associated with
so long were separated from me without the
chance of saying goodbye and we know not
when we shall see them again. How like a
dream all these things are happening, I expect

some day to awake from it. Yang Tsang is now in Canton enjoying his leave of absence with his family. Liang Tun-yen is in Tientsin teaching the telegraph school boys the rudiments of English. Tsai Shou-kee is an assistant translator of the Taotai in Tientsin. They receive twelve and ten taels respectively. Woo Yang-tsang expects to go to the K'ai P'ing mines, and the rest of the boys are distributed in various places to finish (?) their education, not according to their predilections nor to the course they had been pursuing in America, but more in accordance with the wishes of the Chinese Officials whose ignorance and stupidity render them unfit to judge in such matters. . .

In the above excerpts, we can already detect the usual and typical scorn which the "returned student" came to display for the conventional mandarin-official. In turn this scorn was more than balanced by the old type officials' dislike and distrust of these "foreign Chinese". Both had to adjust themselves to each other, but it was a painful and slow process.

Wong was more lucky than most of his fellow students, for he became a translator in the office of the Shanghai Taotai or City Magistrate. As such he received ten taels per month, about the salary of an ordinary office clerk. Most of the students, when they first returned to China, received only four taels monthly, or a little better than the wages of a coolie.

When the shock of their rude reception had somewhat abated, the students of the Mission comforted themselves by attributing their treatment to the stupidity of the local Shanghai officials. They pinned their hopes upon Yung Wing, who had gone to Peking to further their interests. But they soon found that Peking was as indifferent to them as Shanghai had been. In fact, the Imperial Government seems to have made no provision whatsoever either for continuing their education or for placing them in the service of the government in positions where their American education and technical training would be useful. Li Hung-chang, still Viceroy of Chihli, seems to have been the only official of any prominence who realized their capabilities and who took steps to prevent them from being lost among the great host of petty Chinese officials or, even worse, of finding no greater use for their long training in America than to become clerks in the foreign commercial houses in Shanghai. He soon undertook to distribute them among the technical colleges and institutions which he had established in Tientsin. Many were sent to the Naval College and Torpedo School at Tientsin. Others went to the Telegraph School there. Some were attached to the hospital which Li had founded, and several were sent to the K'ai P'ing coal mines north of Tientsin.

Only a very few left the government service in order to take advantage of the opportunities their command of English opened up to them among the foreign firms in the coastal cities.

When the students first returned they had great hopes that the Chinese Government would reverse its policy and send them abroad again to finish the professional courses upon which so many had just embarked. Yung Wing returned to China with the students and attempted to persuade the conservative court officials to this end. He was unsuccessful and as a consequence many of the students were never able to render real professional services to China as engineers. Their training limited them to being skilled artisans. Some rose above this status, and, in such cases as Jeme Tien Yau, became China's first engineers and railroad builders. Others soon forsook the engineering profession for diplomacy or politics and in these fields they made for themselves distinguished and useful careers. This was particularly true of the small group that attached themselves to Yüan Shih-K'ai and went to Korea with him in 1884.

Some few of them were able to create their own careers. Liang Tun-yen, Tong Shao-yi, Tsai Ting-kan, Liang Yu-ho, and a few others were such men, but most of the students had to be content to find their careers in the service of some great official who could use their abilities to promote his own schemes of reform. Li Hung-chang made great use of them, as did his successor, Yüan Shih-k'ai. Tso Tsung-t'ang and Chang Chih-tung employed several of them to further their railway and other projects. Gradually other progressive Viceroys and Governors realized the assistance these young men with their exceptional experience and training could render in the ever increasing problem of dealing with foreigners and in carrying out various industrial, mining, railroad, and telegraph schemes. Such forward looking officials were increasing and many of the students of the Mission were able to exercise a marked influence upon the course of affairs in China as secretaries, interpreters, advisors, and engineers in the employ of these officials.

When the Mission was recalled, Yung Wing resigned his post as Assistant Chinese Minister at Washington to follow his beloved students back to China. At first he attempted to get the Chinese Government to permit at least some of the more advanced students to return to America to finish their technical training, but finding everywhere an indifference to the whole subject of the Educational Mission and feeling that his usefulness to China had ended, in 1883, he returned to his wife and family in Hartford, Connecticut. Arriving home, he found his wife in very poor health, but she recovered for a short time after his return. In 1886 she died, leaving Yung Wing with the care and education of their two sons. Between 1883 and 1895, Yung Wing gave up all connection with the Chinese Government. He was comparatively well off, having conserved the tidy fortune he had made in the tea trade in the early days in China. His style of living in Hartford, although not ostentatious, was on the level of the well-to-do citizens around him. He seems to have been quite popular among his neighbors and fellow-citizens and to have been accepted among them without any manifestations of race prejudice. In 1895 his quiet way of living was unexpectedly interrupted by a call to return to China. The misfortunes of China in the war with Japan, which was going on at this time, had aroused his sympathies and he had forwarded to Chang Chih-tung, the Viceroy of Hunan and Hupeh provinces, a plan to raise a $15,000,000 loan from British bankers. The funds were to be used to provide China with modern armament, and Yung Wing offered to proceed to England to negotiate the loan. Chang Chih-tung accepted his offer and Yung proceeded to London. He had little difficulty in negotiating the loan, but it was never completed because the London bankers insisted that the Chinese customs should be hypothecated to the service of the loan. Li Hung-chang and Sir Robert Hart, who was Inspector General of Customs, refused to give their consent to such demand and the loan fell through. One of the factors that complicated the situation was the bitter political rivalry between Li Hung-chang and Chang Chih-tung. As neither would consent to any plan proposed by the other, Yung Wing's scheme to aid China was frustrated.

One result of this incident was that Chang Chih-tung cabled Yung Wing to return to China. Yung Wing hopefully expected that this great official, who now stood at the apex of his power, would provide him with ample opportunities to put into execution many plans he had in mind for the reform of the outmoded Chinese political and economic set-up. He therefore hastened to obey this summons. The times seemed favorable for the launching of the long postponed but greatly needed program of reforms. China's disastrous defeat in the war with Japan had revealed to all, except those who chose deliberately to blind themselves to the most obvious facts, that if China were to be saved from even greater disasters things could no longer go on in their old slip-shod way. There was talk in the air of the partition of China among the greedy Powers. Rebellion was coming into the open in the South and the very foundations of the Manchu dynasty were imperiled. It must have seemed to Yung Wing that under such conditions he would soon have an opportunity to overcome all the disappointments he had suffered in the past when the Educational Mission was abruptly terminated by instigating a series of reform projects much greater than any he had heretofore anticipated. But again he was to be disappointed.

When he arrived in China, he found that Chang Chih-tung was a very different individual from Tsêng Kuo-fan, the Viceroy with whom he had planned and carried out the Educational Mission. Chang was a cold, supercilious individual who did not warm to Yung Wing's enthusiastic plans for reform. In fact, after inviting him to return to China, Chang Chih-tung did no more than to give Yung Wing an appointment as Secretary of Foreign Affairs in the province of Kiangnan. This was an empty honor and Yung Wing soon realized that Chang Chih-tung was not disposed to make use of him nor to listen to any of his plans. At the end of three months Yung, therefore, resigned his post and proceeded to Shanghai.

He now embarked upon a short career as a free lance reformer. He first suggested to the Peking Government a comprehensive scheme for establishing a National Bank. In this project, he won the support of many powerful officials, but despite this support, Yung Wing's project for a National Bank was defeated by the deeply ingrained Chinese habit of using all government projects as opportunities for private gain. Shing Sun-wei, a multi-millionaire who had a finger in every official pie at this period, hurried to Peking and by a judicious distribution of handsome bribes was able to defeat the scheme and to substitute one more favorable to his own interests.

Yung Wing next proposed a government-built railroad between the port of Tientsin in the North and the port of Chinkiang, near the mouth of the Yangtze. In this he was defeated by the protests of the German Government, which refused to permit the railroad to be built across Shangtung, a province in which it claimed German nationals had a prior right to construct all railroads.

In September, 1898, the Emperor Kuang Hsü attempted to throw off the domination of his aunt, the old Empress Dowager, and, with the aid of such reformers as K'ang Yu-wei and Liang Chi-ch'ao, to accomplish the modernization of China through numerous decrees abolishing the old examination system and eliminating from the government many obsolete features. The Emperor's plans were defeated and it became dangerous for anyone who stood for reform to remain in Peking. Yung Wing, who had been associated with the reformers, had to flee for his life to the safety of the International Concession in Shanghai. His life being still threatened, he then fled to Hong Kong where he stayed for some time, hoping that the moment would come when he could still serve China, but that moment never came. Finally in 1902 he returned to the United States, there to remain until his death in 1911.

The life of Yung Wing graphically illustrates the difficulties and disappointments which were the lot of the first Chinese who attempted to lead China along the paths of modernization. At first, treated as an alien, he was shunned by his own people. Later, when the Educational Mission attained a certain degree of success, his plans were frustrated through the intricacies of Chinese politics. Always he had to fight against the financial corruption with which Chinese officialdom was honeycombed. Nevertheless, Yung Wing did not fail. He, more than any other one person, prepared the ground for China's advances in science and technology. His proteges, the students of the Educational Mission, were the active leaders in establishing modern communications in China. They built railroads, constructed telegraph lines, developed coal mines, became

China's first modern trained army and navy officers, and filled the ranks of her consular and diplomatic service.

Overlooking those who died either in the United States or shortly after they returned to China, the careers of the hundred young Chinese lads who were recalled in 1881 follow these general lines: thirteen of them served in the diplomatic service of China; six spent most of their lives in connection with the great Kailan coal mining administration; fourteen of them were either chief engineers or served in managerial capacities on China's newly constructed railroads; seventeen were naval officers, seven of whom were killed in action and two of whom became admirals in the Imperial Navy; fifteen were identified with the Government Telegraph administration; four practiced medicine; three were connected with China's new educational institutions; two served in the Customs service; twelve followed the more traditional routine careers of the old style Chinese officials, becoming magistrates, taotais, governors, etc. Only ten succumbed to the temptations to forsake the government service for private business; five returned to the United States, and two served in the Consular service of the United States in China.

In all the above capacities, they were the first Chinese to follow these careers. Their technical training placed them in a different category altogether from the old-style Confucian trained officials whose knowledge of the classics was supposed to fit them for any task that the government might command them to undertake. These newcomers were eyed with dislike and suspicion by most of the old mandarinate, but the need for their knowledge gave them many opportunities to direct important enterprises. As a group, with few exceptions, they never rose far up the ladder of official preferment. The old official class was not yet ready to accept them as equals, and everything was done to keep them in the lower ranks of the nine official titles. In a sense, the advent of the republic in 1912 was a misfortune for them. They were now past the prime of life and carried with them the stigma of having served under the old Imperial regime. Moreover, by 1912, the numbers of foreign trained students had greatly increased and young men, with no previous political affiliations to be held against them, now received positions that should have crowned the careers of this pioneer group of China's first returned students.

CHAPTER V

VICEROYS AS ADMIRALS: CHINA'S FIRST NAVIES

Necessity caused China's earliest reformers to turn to the problem of providing an adequate system of coast defense, for it was the coastal provinces which first experienced the destructive power of modern arms and shells. In fact, it was this side of China's military weakness, made woefully apparent in the Sino-British Opium War of 1840, which forced such early reformers as Lin Tsê-hsü and Tso Tsung-t'ang to turn their attention to the whole problem of introducing into China the military and naval armaments of the Occident. As early as 1840, Lin Tsê-hsü, who, as Special Commissioner of the Emperor at Canton, had to devise the best means of defending the coast against the attacks of the British naval squadron, began to manufacture cannon by methods he had learned from various foreigners. In the *Hai Kuo t'u Chih* or *Illustrated Record of the Maritime Nations*, which was published under Lin's patronage in 1844, Lin openly admitted the superiority of Western arms over the antiquated spears and bows of the Imperial troops, and he warmly advocated the adoption of them as quickly as possible. China having lost the war, Lin philosophically concluded: "Let us now, in this time of peace, adopt the superior skill of the barbarians in order to control them with greater effect . . . The barbarians are superior in three ways: firstly, warships; secondly, firearms; and thirdly, methods of military training and discipline of soldiers . . . Let us build a dock and an arsenal at Sha Chiao and Ta Chiao . . . One or two 'barbarian eyes' [experts] from France and America should be invited to bring foreign artisans to Canton to supervise the construction of ships and to manufacture firearms."

These daring proposals of Lin, which ran counter to the overwhelming prejudice against the foreigners permeating the official world of China, were written while Lin was still in Chinese Turkestan, where he had been banished because of his failure to keep the British from invading the sacred soil of the Middle Kingdom. As we might well guess, nothing came of Lin's proposals. China had to suffer another great disaster before several of the Viceroys summoned enough courage to brook the prejudice around them and began to experiment with the manufacture of foreign arms and ammunition. The great T'ai P'ing rebellion, which raged in central China from 1850 to 1865, gave a great impetus to the many desultory attempts to begin the modernizations of China's weapons of defense.

The first arsenal and shipyard of any importance to be established in China seems to have been set up at Anking by Tsêng Kuo-fan in 1861 during the final phases of his campaign against the T'ai P'ing rebels. At the Anking arsenal Tsêng manufactured cannon and ammunition and he began his first experiments in the construction of a small steam vessel. These experiments were crowned with success when, on January 28, 1863, Tsêng took a short trip on a steamer made by his mechanics at Anking.

The next arsenal to be constructed was the one at Soochow which Li Hung-chang built in 1864 just after he recaptured this city from the T'ai P'ings. Its superintendent was the English military surgeon, Sir Haliday Macartney, who at this time was in the service of Li Hung-chang. Shortly after its establishment the arsenal was moved to Nanking, where it was located near the Yu Hua Tai, the famous porcelain tower, which in those days stood just south of the city walls.

In 1864 Tsêng Kuo-fan, wishing to extend the work being done at Anking, established the famous Kiangnan arsenal and dockyard on the outskirts of Shanghai. Originally, the dockyard had belonged to Tom Falls, an enterprising Englishman. Tsêng

Kuo-fan bought this establishment at the end of the T'ai P'ing rebellion and later, with the help of Yung Wing, converted it into a naval dockyard and engineering school. The first steam-vessel to be built at the Kiangnan Arsenal was completed in 1865. It was constructed by Hsu Shou, one of Tsêng Kuo-fan's mechanics, who got his ideas for the design of the steamer from studying the drawings and descriptions of steam engines in Dr. Benjamin Hobson's small encyclopedia of natural philosophy. This work, published in Chinese in 1855, was one of the pioneer compendiums in which the Chinese were first enabled to study the scientific knowledge of the Occidental nations. When completed the steamer displaced about twenty-five tons and on her first trip on the Yangtze made a run of about 85 miles in fourteen hours. Tsêng was delighted at the success of the experiment and it greatly encouraged him to go on to more ambitious projects. How his enthusiasm for foreign ships and guns led to his sending for Yung Wing and the latter's dispatch to the United States to purchase the machinery for the Kiangnan Arsenal has been already related.

The first steamer to be built in China, other than the small experimental ones built at Anking in 1863 and at Kiangnan in 1865, was launched from the Kiangnan Arsenal docks in September, 1868. When Tsêng took his first ride in the vessel, he was so delighted with it that he named the boat the Tien Chih, or Calm and Prosperous, meaning thereby, as he explained in a report to the Throne, that the four seas were calm and the machine shops at Kiangnan were prosperous. The Tien Chih was one-hundred and eight-five feet long and twenty-seven and one half-feet wide. Before Tsêng's death in 1871, five large steamers had been built at Kiangnan. The arsenal continued into the twentieth century to be a center of ship construction for the Chinese Government. In addition, in the printing shop attached to the arsenal there were translated and published between 1868 and 1882 over two hundred standard scientific works. In its shops thousands of Chinese labourers were trained in ship construction, machine operation, steel fabrication, and the many other skills which go into the construction of a modern steam vessel. Thus Tsêng Kuo-fan's hopes that the arsenal would become a center where the Chinese could gradually master the technical arts were amply fulfilled.

Mention has already been made of another noteworthy attempt to initiate the Chinese into the arts of shipbuilding and navigation which was launched at about the same time that Tsêng Kuo-fan established the Kiangnan Arsenal. This was the Foochow Arsenal and Naval School established in 1866 by Tso Tsung-t'ang, the Viceroy of Fukien province. In 1877, when Prosper Giquel, the chief engineer, was ready to return to France, Tso Tsung-t'ang requested him to take to Europe with him some thirty graduates of the Naval School. In Europe, the Governments of Great Britain and France invited these young Chinese to enter their naval colleges, and they were given opportunities to serve on British and French warships. At the end of three years, they returned to China to become teachers in the various arsenals and technical schools established in the coastal provinces.

These efforts to establish a modern naval service in China suffered from the peculiar political system whereby all these early attempts were left entirely to the individual initiative and enthusiasm of the Viceroys of the coastal provinces. Each Viceroy considered his fleet as being limited to the defense of the two provinces which made up his viceroyalty. Under these circumstances there gradually developed a series of fleets of greatly varying degrees of efficiency and modernization. The Viceroy of the two southernmost provinces of Kuangtung and Kuangsi had his fleet based upon Canton. The Viceroy of Fukien province also had his fleet, which was stationed at Foochow. The Nan Yang Hai Chun, or Southern Seas squadron, was controlled by the Viceroy at Nanking, while the Pei Yang Hai Chun, or

Northern Seas Squadron, was under the direct command of Li Hung-chang. As Viceroy of the Metropolitan province of Chihli, Li's squadron was more nearly a national force than any of the other fleets, for it was concerned with the defense of the province which contained the center of Imperial administration and the residence of the Emperor at Peking. But in every detail connected with its creation and administration Li enjoyed full authority. In fact, the funds for the purchase and construction of vessels were derived from the provincial revenues. Strange as this system might appear to the foreigner, it appeared perfectly logical to the Chinese who well understood the political theory underlying such an arrangement. By this system, the responsibility for the success or failure of such ventures rested upon the shoulders of the Viceroys, who, in turn, well understood that they would be held fully responsible if these ventures into "barbarian" learning failed of their purpose. The political convenience of this device was well demonstrated in the Sino-Japanese War of 1895, when Li Hung-chang's fleet of modern cruisers was completely defeated by the better prepared Japanese navy. The Imperial Government neatly escaped all blame for the disaster by degrading Li Hung-chang, stripping him of all his honors, and dismissing him from office. The censure of the nation thus was centered upon Li rather than upon the Emperor and his advisors.

Under the circumstances described above, the students of the Educational Mission, who upon their return to China were assigned to the Naval School at Foochow and the various institutions at Tientsin connected with Li Hung-chang's growing Northern squadron, could not look forward to careers in a truly national navy. In fact, if it had not been for the determination of Li Hung-chang to make use of them in his own fleet, it is doubtful that any of them would have been enabled to follow naval careers at all. It was this desire of Li to use them as the nucleus of a corps of technically trained officers which caused him to be indifferent to the recall of the Mission in 1881. He had just established the Naval College at Tientsin and a Torpedo School at Taku. These institutions had been placed in the charge of competent foreign experts, and a curriculum of studies had been drawn up which was greatly superior to the purely mechanical training which had been provided at the schools attached to the various arsenals. In these latter places very little attempt had been made to carry the students beyond the practical engineering connected with the construction and operation of steam vessels. In the Naval College at Tientsin, provision was made for a thorough theoretical training to support the more practical training in the various branches of the naval profession. The Naval College and Torpedo School were just ready to receive students when the Educational Mission was recalled from the United States.

Several years earlier, the Imperial Government had attempted to organize a navy along modern lines. In 1863, eight gunboats were purchased in England and brought to China by Captain Osburne of the British Navy. A misunderstanding arose between Captain Osburne and the Chinese Government as to the command of this fleet with the unfortunate result that the boats were sold and the attempt to establish a navy was given up. The facts of the situation were that the Viceroys would not relinquish their traditional control over the military and naval forces of China, and they combined to defeat the plan for a navy under the direct command of the Imperial Government at Peking.

When Li Hung-chang became Viceroy of Chihli in 1871, he immediately began plans to purchase a fleet of modern war vessels. Little progress was made, however, until after the war between France and China which lasted from 1881 to 1885. At the end of the war two iron clad battleships which Li had purchased in England arrived in the Far East and became the nucleus of the Northern Squadron. By 1894, at the outbreak of the war with Japan, the Northern squadron consisted of some twenty modern ships of war, two of which were heavy cruisers, the rest light cruisers and gunboats. In the combined fleets of all the viceroyalties there were about ninety-five vessels of greatly varying size and efficiency but only the Northern fleet of Li Hung-chang actually fought the Japanese. The southern viceroys kept their fleets safely in the shelter of their ports, unconcerned with what they considered to be Li's private quarrel with Japan.

Most of the students of the Mission who were designated for careers in the navy either were assigned to the squadron at Foochow or joined the Northern squadron at Tientsin. The group sent to the Naval College at Foochow were the first to experience an actual clash between China's new navy and the fleet of a European power. This occurred in 1884 at the Battle of Pagoda Anchorage off Foochow, when the French fleet under Admiral Courbet, without any previous indications of hostile intentions, opened fire upon the Chinese squadron. The sole motive for the attack seems to have been the desire of the French to restore the prestige French arms had suffered when, some months before, a French attack upon the Sino-Tonking border post of Langsan had been repulsed by the Chinese. The French fleet was composed of eight heavily armoured cruisers, whereas the Chinese fleet consisted of eleven ships, only two of which were armoured, the other nine being converted wooden junks. The Chinese commander was totally unprepared for the attack as the French had been peacefully anchored nearby for more than a month. Suddenly the French opened fire and within a few minutes the Chinese vessels were totally destroyed or rendered helpless. The French then proceeded to bombard the Foochow Arsenal, erected some years before under the supervision of the French engineer, Prosper Giquel, and which stood as a tribute to the engineering efficiency of the French. Its splendid docks and workshops were soon in ruins, and in a few moments it was transformed from a monument of peaceful cultural interchange between China and the West into a symbol of unrestrained imperialistic aggression.

Six of the Chinese vessels were commanded by former students of the Educational Mission. Despite the obvious hopelessness of their position, they fought back as long as it was possible to do so. The result was that four out of the six lost their lives in this action. The four whose lives were thus sacrificed were Kwong Wing-chung, Sit Yau-fu, Yang Sew-nan, and Wong Kwei-liang. Another of the former students, Captain Yung Leang, now living in retirement in Shanghai and who is still known among his intimates by his American name of "By-Jinks Johnnie", relates his experiences at the Battle of Pagoda Anchorage. He says: "The magazine of the ship to which I was attached blew up and she went to the bottom and I into the water. After I swam to the shore, I made my way to the hill back of the anchorage to be out of the firing, for the ships were all destroyed, the enemy shelling the Arsenal, docks and building yards. Not being used to go barefooted and being slightly wounded in the left foot, it was a torture to go about on account of the sharp stones. In order to swim, I had kicked off my shoes. That night I passed in a deserted hut on the bank of the river. The next morning I came across a few soldiers cooking rice and I helped myself to a few handfuls. My feet were getting so sore, I could hardly stand on them, so I went to a tree and sat at its foot the whole day and with an empty stomach. Not a soul was in sight as all the people had fled.

"When daylight came on the next morning, I made my way to the bank of the river where I found a sampan loaded with wounded bound for the city of Foochow. I got on board and when we were abreast of the arsenal I landed and went to the authorities to get my three months arrears of pay amounting to $33. Instead of that sum, I was given $3, with the remark "We have no money." Of course I was bitterly disappointed

74

but as I was absolutely destitute, I took it and made my way to Foochow about twelve miles away. The only person I knew there was a Chinese Educational Mission boy who was in the Telegraph service, but he was out inspecting the line. With the $3 I bought a cotton suit, a pair of shoes and the necessary toilet articles. At the end I had eight cents left over. With this wealth I bought a big bag of peanuts and sat on the curb of a Foochow city street, finished the nuts and got a free drink of tea from the shop where I bought the peanuts."

The American Minister to China at the time used the Pagoda Anchorage episode to bring to the notice of the Chinese Government the desire of the American Government to see China resume the practice of sending students to America. He praised the bravery which the American educated students exhibited during the course of the French attack and said that it disproved the belief that the students had become so westernized that they could be of little service to China. He said their heroism under fire made it "manifestly evident that they had done great service to China, and that their education in the United States had not proved fruitless."

Ten years later in the war between Japan and China the former students of the Mission again demonstrated their coolness and courage in battle. At the disastrous engagement of Yalu, off the Manchurian coast, three of them lost their lives while vainly struggling to resist superior Japanese forces. The officers who died in this engagement were Chin Kin-kwai, commander of the cruiser "Chi Yuen"; Shen Shao-chang, who commanded the "Tsai Yuen", the sister ship of the "Chi Yuen"; and Wong Chu-lin, captain of the light cruiser "Kwong Ping."

A few weeks later, at the siege of Weihaiwei, the Japanese succeeded in destroying the remnants of Li's fine cruiser squadron. Li Hung-chang met a just retribution in the disaster of the Sino-Japanese war as he was directly responsible for the sorry showing of the Northern fleet. Li, whose greed for money was notorious, had allowed the effectiveness of the fleet to become undermined by a vast system of peculation. In fact, at the time of the Battle of Yalu, his fine appearing squadron of modern cruisers was little more than a hollow sham. The ships went into battle with only a pitiful supply of ammunition for the big guns, and ammunition of very doubtful quality for the smaller arms. It was suspected at the time that the Empress Dowager, Tz'u Hsi, was party to the system of corruption which had diverted the immense sums set aside for the navy to personal and other unworthy ends. Great sums were thus squandered in order that Old Buddha, as the Empress Dowager was popularly called, might have the satisfaction of building a vast new Summer Palace to replace the one destroyed by the French and British in 1860. The American educated students who served as officers in this navy were quite aware of the peculation which was ruining the fighting strength of the modern cruisers and battleships. Yet there was nothing they could do to stem the tide of corruption. Many of them left the navy in disgust, but those who stayed distinguished themselves by their bravery and devotion to duty. They also kept themselves aloof from the evil politics around them. Nevertheless, their situation was difficult and unpleasant. We catch a glimpse of this in the sympathetic references to Admiral Woo Ying-fo in W. E. Tyler's interesting book, *Pulling Strings in China*. Tyler was one of the foreign instructors attached to the Northern squadron at the outbreak of the Sino-Japanese war. He served on the flagship "Ting Yuen" with Woo, who at that time was Flag Lieutenant of the fleet. The two young officers, both standing aloof from what Tyler well describes as "the enervating permeance of mandarinism", were drawn together in a strong friendship.

The seige of Weihaiwei, where the Japanese had bottled up the remnants of the Chinese fleet, marked the final scene of China's naval tragedy. When capitulation became unavoidable, Admiral Ting Ju-chang, who had command of the Northern squadron, took the time-honoured way out of the situation by committing suicide. In this way, the lives of many of his subordinate officers were saved from the vengeance of the Imperial Court. Captain Yung Leang served on the flagship during the siege and was an eye witness of the events which took place in the last few days of Chinese resistance. He relates some very illuminating incidents of the final act of that tragedy. He says that when Admiral Ting, who had been an old time cavalry officer in the Imperial army before being arbitrarily assigned to command the Northern squadron, was making his preparations to commit suicide he called six carpenters to make a coffin for him. When it was finished he got into the coffin and rolled his shoulders around to see if it was satisfactory. Tipping the carpenters $2 each, he bade farewell to his officers and retired to his cabin to take the fatal dose of poison. In contrast to the action of Admiral Ting, which was in perfect keeping with the old Chinese tradition, the American trained Flag Lieutenant, Woo Ying-fu, filled with disgust at the political corruption which had caused the defeat of the fleet, wrapped all his decorations and the button of rank in his mandarin's cap and threw them into the sea.

There is no doubt that the ex-American students had a lonely row to hoe amidst the mandarinism of the decaying Manchu regime. To their everlasting honor, they stuck to it almost to a man, and most often to the detriment of their own personal fortunes and official careers.

The overwhelming defeat suffered by China at the hands of Japan in the war of 1895 marked a change in the fortunes of the Educational Mission students. Up to this time they had been treated with little more consideration than yamen clerks and coolie mechanics. Their willingness to work with their hands and actually to engage in the construction and operation of engines caused them to be greatly despised by the scholar-officials. Very few of them had been able to get beyond the lowest official ranks, and even in the navy they had been forced to take positions inferior to the officials who, without any technical qualifications whatsoever, were appointed to the upper ranks. But after 1895, even the most reactionary mandarins were brought to a sense of reality by the shock of defeat inflicted upon China by the much despised Japanese. Memorial after memorial was sent up to the Throne pointing out the moral of the defeat and pleading with the Throne to follow Japan's example in mastering the learning of the Westerners. Nearly all these memorials proposed that railways be introduced into China as rapidly as possible in order to strengthen the nation against further attack. The Imperial government was at last ready to set its face towards reform and to give up its empty pose of despising the foreigners and the foreigners' technological skill. Many railway and mining schemes were begun after 1895 and in a very short while the American trained students were called upon to execute such projects. Now they advanced rapidly up the scale of official promotion as they were entrusted with increasingly important tasks. Nowhere was this new attitude towards them better shown than in the naval service. By 1911, when the Manchu regime ended, two admirals and one Vice-Minister of the Navy emerged from the ranks of the former students of the Educational Mission.

One of those who attained the rank of Admiral was Tsai Ting-kan. His death in September, 1935, removed one of the most picturesque figures from the stage of modern Chinese politics. During his stay in America he took on American ways and speech with great facility. He was a very witty after-dinner speaker and was one of the best known Chinese among the foreign community in China. As a young boy in America, his companions dubbed him "Fighting Chinee". He got this nickname because of his peculiar penchant for getting into mischief. In fact, Mrs. MacLean, in whose home he lived in Springfield, Massachusetts, advised the Chinese Commissioners at Hartford to send him home as she believed that he would never profit from a long period of study in America. But young Tsai was a general favorite and instead of sending him back to China it was arranged that he should be sent to Lowell, Massachusetts, to learn practical machinery in the machine shops there. While at Lowell, he obtained permission to cut off his pigtail because of the danger to which it exposed him while working around the rapidly moving machinery.

Upon his return to China, in 1881, he was assigned to the Torpedo School at Taku, near Tientsin. Here he received a thorough training in the management of torpedos and torpedo boats from Major Mannix, the foreign instructor of the school. In 1884 he was appointed Lieutenant, with Fifth Class Naval honors, and assigned to the Northern Seas Squadron. Tsai thus escaped the treacherous attack of the French upon the helpless Chinese fleet at Pagoda Anchorage. In 1890 he was placed in command of the squadron of torpedo boats which had just been purchased in Europe by Li Hung-chang. At the outbreak of the Sino-Japanese war, his squadron was attached to Port Arthur, but after its capture by the Japanese, Admiral Tsai escaped to Weihaiwei, where the Northern fleet was concentrated for a last stand. In this battle Tsai distinguished himself by his bravery and coolness in action. Despite a painful wound caused by a shell splinter, he remained on his ship until it was on the verge of sinking beneath him. He then jumped into the sea and was captured by the Japanese.

The story has been told above how the Empress Dowager, whose greed and extravagance were in no small measure responsible for the pitiful supplies of ammunition with which the ships went into action, shifted responsibility for the disaster to the shoulders of Li Hung-chang and the officers of the fleet. Tsai, together with the rest, was degraded in rank and lost all of his honors. He did not have his rank and honors restored to him until 1908, when Yüan Shih-k'ai petitioned the Throne for their restoration. From this time on Tsai's rise in rank was very rapid, for Yüan took a great liking to him and admired his wit and outspoken manner. When Yüan was dismissed from office after the death of the Empress Dowager, Tsai also retired, but when, in 1911, Yüan returned to power one of his first acts was to make Tsai Ting-kan an admiral and to place him in charge of naval affairs.

Unlike most of the former students of the Mission, Tsai survived the political chaos which characterized Republican politics. During Yüan's Shih-k'ai's tenure as President of the Republic, Tsai acted as Adviser to Yüan and, after the latter's death, he served in various capacities connected with the Salt Administration and the Maritime Customs. The successive warlords who from time to time dominated the Chinese scene delighted in bestowing elaborate decorations upon him. The result was that Tsai became the most decorated man in China. For a time he served as Minister of Ceremonies to the abdicated emperor, Hsüan Tung, who after the revolution of 1911 continued to live in the Forbidden City in Peking. In 1925 he was one of the three commissioners sent to investigate the May 30th shooting affray, in which the police of the International Concession of Shanghai fired upon parading Chinese students. Shortly after this he was commissioned by the President of the Republic to be Minister of Foreign Affairs, but he seems never to have taken up this post. About this time he retired from public life, living part of the time in Darien and part of the time in Peking. He died in Peking on September 29th, 1935. In his last years he dabbled in Chinese scholarship, priding himself upon his studies of ancient calligraphy. He translated into English rhyme some 120 poems of the T'ang and Sung dynasty. He was also very much interested in the concept of the "gentleman" as it evolved during the Confucian period of Chinese history. He gathered extensive materials from the classics through which he wanted to show the evolution of the central Confucian concept of the "chun tzê" or "princely man". In his own words, the aim of this work was "to place before the eyes and mind of the Chinese youth the Confucian ideal and conception of the "chun tzê". In these activities of his old age, he seemed to be reaching back across the ages to the source of traditional Chinese culture from which the American education of his youth had cut him off.

The other naval student who rose to the rank of admiral was Woo Ying-fu, who was Flag Lieutenant on the cruiser "Ting Yuen" at the time of the Battle of Yalu. He was sent to the United States in 1875 and for five years lived in the home of the Reverend A. G. Loomis at Greenfield, Massachusetts. From Greenfield, he was sent to Andover Academy for two years and then to Rensselaer Polytechnic Institute. At the end of one year at this institution, he returned home with the others of the Mission upon its recall. He was sent to the Foochow Naval School where he stayed for two years before being assigned to active duty in the Northern Squadron. Woo was more fortunate than most of the officers of the ill-fated Northern fleet, for he escaped being degraded after the disasters of Yalu and Weihaiwei. Instead he was decorated for bravery and advanced in rank. In 1899 he was appointed to accompany the Special Delegation which was sent to England to attend the coronation of King Edward VII. From 1901 to 1908 he was in command of the Kiangnan Arsenal dockyards, and in 1908 he was appointed Admiral of the cruiser squadron. After the advent of the republic, he served as Minister of Communications and then as Admiral under Yüan Shih-k'ai. In 1916 he resigned his offices and he now lives in quiet retirement in Peking.

In many ways, the students who were sent to the navy after their return to China had the most difficult task. They were surrounded on every side by peculation and inefficiency. Their commanding officers, with few exceptions, were political appointees without any qualifications for the posts they held.

Seven of them sacrificed their lives, not so much in defense of their country, but because of the maze of wholesale dishonesty which permeated official China under the dying Manchu regime. Surrounded on every side by an enervating atmosphere of social decay, Yung Wing's "Americans" had to fight against a well-nigh hopeless situation to accomplish what they did in bringing about a rejuvenated modern China.

CHAPTER VI

Tien Hsien or Threads of Lightning

The introduction of the telegraph into China was another innovation which may be attributed to Li Hung-chang. In 1879 he built a short line to connect his headquarters at Tientsin with the forts at Taku Bar at the mouth of the Peiho river. His chief object in constructing this line was to demonstrate to the Court the practical utility of the telegraph in conveying military commands and in the mobilization of troops. The experiment convinced a somewhat doubtful Court and shortly thereafter orders were given to construct a line between Peking and Shanghai. In the next ten years lines were erected linking most of the provincial capitals with Peking. In fact, the building of telegraph lines encountered scarcely any of the obstacles which were met with in the attempts to introduce railroads and to develop mines in China. For one thing, the construction of telegraph lines did not involve the large outlay of capital required by railways and mines. The necessary capital could easily be raised by the provincial governments. Once the lines were built, the revenues from them soon returned their initial cost to the government. The cost of building railroads required such large amounts of capital that the Chinese Government had either to secure the necessary funds through foreign loans or had to grant outright concessions to foreign interest to finance and construct the lines. Either method imposed limitations upon Chinese sovereignty and permitted the obnoxious foreigner to penetrate into the interior of the country. Moreover, both railroads and mines required the services of foreign engineers and financial experts who demanded large salaries and who had a tendency to bring the diplomatic pressure of their respective governments to bear whenever any difference arose between themselves and the Chinese Government. Hardly ever could the Chinese Government treat such foreign experts as mere employees. Nearly always they had to be employed under the euphemous title of "advisers" which gave them a semi-diplomatic status.

Telegraph lines could be built without encountering such difficulties. The initial outlay of capital was small and once the lines were built their operation entailed a minimum of foreign aid. Chinese telegraph operators could be easily trained and there were sufficient western trained students of the Educational Mission to fill the managerial posts. The telegraph was one western technique which the Chinese could safely keep in their own hands and therefore there was little opposition to the introduction of an instrument of such obvious utility. Furthermore, the telegraph greatly increased the control of the Imperial Government over provincial officials, which caused the Court to encourage the building of lines connecting Peking with the provincial capitals. In great contrast to its attitude towards the telegraph, the Court resolutely resisted all attemps to bring the railway into Peking. It was not until the Boxer Rebellion gave the foreigners the opportunity to have their way that they forcibly breached the city's walls and extended the railway to the main entrance of the Forbidden City.

Li Hung-chang's telegraph line between Tientsin and the Taku forts was actually not the first telegraph line to be built in China. It was, however, the first to be voluntarily and freely built solely upon Chinese initiative. The first lines were forced upon the Chinese by aggressive foreigners in much the same spirit that one might force a child to take medicine "for its own good". In fact, the circumstances under which the telegraph was first brought into China is very illuminating in that it serves admirably to illustrate how the foreigners were determined to impose western progress upon China whether the Chinese wanted it or not. It also serves to show how Chinese statesmen, in the light of their background and in what they considered to be the best interests of China, tried to resist the introduction of these "Greek gifts" from the West.

The first attempt to build a telegraph line occurred in 1865, when an Englishman named Reynolds erected a line between Shanghai and the port of Woosung, some twelve miles distant. He thought to make a fortune by notifying the foreign and Chinese firms of the arrival of vessels off the mouth of the Yangtze. But the people living along the lines, no doubt encouraged by the local officials, removed the poles and stole the copper wire. In the same year, the American and Russian ministers in Peking had made naive attempts to interest the Court in the telegraph. Anson Burlingame, the American minister and a noted enthusiast for the westernization of China, gave Prince Kung, who headed the Government, a long lecture upon the principles and operation of the telegraph. The Russian Minister, hearing about it and not to be outdone, sent for a complete model telegraph system which he caused to be erected in the compound of the Russian Legation. He then invited Prince Kung and the other leading officials to a demonstration in which messages were sent and received in Chinese. Both ministers were politely thanked by the Court but nothing came of their efforts.

The next attempt came when the Great Northern Telegraph Company, a Danish concern, tried to connect its cable, which ran along the coast between Shanghai and Hong Kong, with stations on shore. The cable was laid in 1871 and in the next few years, failing to get permission of the Chinese government to extend the end of the cable at Shanghai to the shore, the Company maintained a receiving station upon a floating hulk off Woosung. But in 1873 the Company, becoming impatient at the constant procrastination on the part of the Chinese Magistrate at Shanghai to give permission to extend the cable to the shore, simply went ahead and made the necessary connections. Immediately the Magistrate protested to the Consular body at this violation of Chinese sovereignty. He also pointed out that some years previously the British Minister had promised that his Government would not countenance any attempts of British subjects to erect telegraph lines on Chinese soil. When the Consular body met to discuss the matter they decided that as the action of the Company could not be defended, the best course would be to ignore the protest of the Chinese Magistrate. At the same time the Consuls gave their tacit approval of the action of the Company by making public a resolution in which they stated that "the telegraph is an appliance, the utility of which cannot be overrated, and against which no arguments worthy of consideration can be adduced." In this case the usefulness of the line was quickly demonstrated as the Chinese merchants at Shanghai began to employ the telegraph to carry on their business with Hong Kong and other ports along the way. The people offered no objection to the line and it was allowed to stand.

A far more serious situation arose, however, when the Great Northern Telegraph Company began to construct a telegraph line between the ports of Foochow and Amoy. In 1874 the Company secured from the Viceroy of Fukien province a concession to build a telegraph line between Foochow and Amoy, a distance of some two hundred miles. Previous to this, the Viceroy had permitted the Company to build a line nine miles long connecting Foochow with the shipping anchorage at the mouth of the Min River.

Evidently in the sheer exuberance of international spirits engendered in bringing western progress to China, Mr. M. De Lano, the American Consul at Foochow, had secured both of these concessions for the Danish Company. The American Minister added the proper touch to this demonstration of international comity by complimenting Mr. De Lano for his zeal in "promoting the interests of civilization and humanity in this vast empire." In the concession agreement, the Chinese provincial authorities reserved the right to purchase the line at cost at any time after it was completed. In fact, it was the evident intention of the Chinese to do this and in granting the concession they merely intended that the Company should build the line. In order to quiet any local opposition that might arise along the route, the contract provided that the line should be built so as not to disturb the roads, graves, houses or fields of the local population. To ensure enforcement of these protective measures the line was surveyed under the direction of a Chinese official. Work was begun but after about eight miles had been built, the local Magistrate through whose jurisdiction the line was being built was transferred to another post and a new magistrate was appointed. The newcomer soon showed that he had no intention of permitting the construction of the line to proceed and he endeavored to persuade the Company to cease construction. He warned the Company that the populace would rise up and destroy the line if work on it were not stopped. These warnings were disregarded and the line was built for a distance for some thirty-five miles. At this point, the villagers began to tear down the poles and to make off with the copper wire, thus bringing construction to a halt. These acts were quite evidently done with the connivance of the local magistrate. What had happened was that the Imperial authorities in Peking had disapproved the action of the previous Magistrate in granting the concession and, after transferring him to another post, now encouraged the people to destroy the line.

The direct action of the local population in stopping work on the line soon set the machinery of Occidental diplomacy in motion in order to protect the legal interests of the Company. The Danish Government appointed General De Raasloff to proceed to Peking to protest to the Imperial government against the violation of the rights of the Telegraph Company. Upon his arrival in Peking, General De Raasloff immediately enlisted the willing aid of his diplomatic colleagues to bring pressure upon the Chinese Government. The ministers of Great Britain, France, Germany, Russia, and the United States, motivated no doubt by *noblesse oblige,* presented a joint protocol to the Imperial Government demanding that it should recognize the rights of the Telegraph Company under the Foochow-Amoy concession. For good measure they also demanded that the Chinese Government should protect the cable which the Company had laid along the China coast and the short cables connecting it with the ports along the way. Faced with this solid diplomatic front, there was nothing for the Chinese officials to do but to give the required assurances. Thus, the illegal actions of the foreign entrepreneurs in connecting the coastal cable with shore stations over the protest of the Chinese Government were not only made legal but the Chinese Government was made responsible for the protection of such cables. General De Raasloff, knowing full well that he could depend upon the support of the entire diplomatic corps in Peking, began to press for a settlement of the Foochow-Amoy concession. The final result was that the Imperial authorities agreed to buy the line outright for $154,000, but $50,000 of this amount represented an indemnity to the Company for the loss of the concession. Mr. Avery, the American Minister, summed up the viewpoint of the foreigners when he reported the "satisfactory" conclusion of the incident by remarking that "If we rest on the assertion that China will be left to advance in her own time and way, and fail to indicate when a good time and way are presented, we are simply allies of the native apathy and inertia which opposed progress now as they have opposed it heretofore."

The Chinese officials were confronted in this instance with the unbeatable combination of Occidental diplomacy and Occidental legalism. They could only protest against the violation of Chinese sovereignty and assert that such innovations as the telegraph, the steamship, and the railroad would upset the age-old balance of Chinese economic life. As a last resort, they encouraged the people to destroy the line. This gave the foreigners the desired legal wedge to force upon China the technology of Occidental progress. The foreigner, resting his case upon his legal rights and inspired by the conviction that such technology could only benefit China, disregarded the precarious balance between life and starvation which had been reached in over-populated China through centuries of trial and error. In his mind, if his telegraphs and railroads and steamships did upset that balance, then "so much the better for China."

By 1889 all the provinces, with the exceptions of Shansi, Kansu, and Hunan, had telegraph lines connecting the provincial capitals with Peking. Hunan, always proud of its conservatism, held out to the last. In 1891, when the Imperial Chinese Telegraph Administration attempted to erect a line within the borders of Hunan, the inhabitants rose en masse and so badly injured the working party and military escort that they had to fly for their lives, abandoning equipment of much value. Several lives were lost in this affair, including that of a local metropolitan graduate who had encouraged the innovation. By 1896, however, the spirit of the people of Hunan had changed and they made no attempt to interfere with the construction of a line connecting Changsha, the capital, with Wuchang.

All these lines were kept under the control of the Chinese Government and were entirely built and staffed by Chinese engineers. These engineers were drawn from the Imperial Northern Government Telegraph College which Li Hung-chang had established at Tientsin in 1879. At this college instruction was offered in telegraph practice, traffic management, rules of international telegraph conventions, electricity and magnetism, construction of land and submarine lines, surveying of routes, and other phases of telegraph engineering. By 1895, some three hundred students had been graduated from this college. The nucleus of the staff of the Imperial Telegraph Administration was formed by the twenty students of the Educational Mission who upon their return to China were assigned to the Telegraph College. So determined was the Chinese government to keep the telegraph system under its control that it was not until 1893 that permission was given to join the Chinese system with the Russian system in Manchuria, thus giving China direct telegraphic connections with the rest of the world. Before this date, telegraphs to and from the interior had to be relayed to the foreign cable systems at the ports.

Of the twenty students of the Educational Mission who were assigned to the telegraph service, a few soon left for more lucrative employments, but most of them stayed with the service until death or retirement ended their careers. When the lines were first built, they were humble telegraph operators, but as time went on they slowly climbed up the ladder of advancement until they had charge of the telegraph administration of whole provinces. In a few instances, former students of the Mission successively held the post of Director General of Telegraphs for all China.

One of the most outstanding members of the Chinese Educational Mission who was connected with the telegraph service was Liang Tun-yen. In 1881, upon his return to China, he was sent to Tientsin to be the teacher of English in the Telegraph College. In 1884 he left this post to become the secretary of Chang Chih-tung, the famous reformer and political rival of Li Hung-chang. At this time, Chang Chih-tung was the Governor General of the two Kuangs, that is the provinces of Kuangtung and Kuangsi. Liang Tun-yen's fortunes rose with those of his chief. In 1908, when Yüan Shih-k'ai went into retirement and Chang Chih-tung took over the leadership of affairs, Liang was appointed Minister of Foreign Affairs. In 1910 he was sent on a special diplomatic mission to Europe, and when in 1911 the revolution broke out, he was recalled by Yüan Shih-k'ai to become Minister of Communications in the first Republican government. In this post, Liang had charge of all forms of communications in China, including railroads, steamship lines, and telegraph and telephone systems.

Wong Kai-kah, who in America earned the nickname of "Breezey Jack" and who had such a gift of eloquence that, as one of his fellow students at Hartford put it, "he could make a fine speech when shaken from a sound slumber without a moment's notice," did not rise to such a prominent place as did Liang Tun-yen. Soon after the return of the students, Shen Kung-pao, the Managing Director of the China Merchant's Steam Navigation Company and a consistent advocate of westernization, recognized Wong's ability and made him his secretary. Later, Shen Kung-pao was placed in charge of Communications and was responsible for pushing to completion some of the early telegraph and railway projects. Without a doubt, he was greatly helped in his various schemes for the modernization of China by Wong Kai-kah. In the latter years of his life, Wong Kai-kah served as Secretary to the various princely envoys which the Chinese Government sent to America and Europe. In 1902 he was Secretary to the embassy sent by the Imperial Government to attend the coronation ceremonies of King Edward VII, and in 1904 he accompanied Prince Pu Lun to the United States, where the prince served as Imperial Commissioner at the St. Louis Exposition. In 1905 he was one of the representatives of China at the Portland Peace Conference which closed the Russo-Japanese war. Unfortunately, on his way home from the Peace Conference, his promising career was cut short by an accident in which he lost his life.

Tong Yuen-chan was another of the Hartford boys who slowly advanced in the telegraph service until he finally became Director General of the Imperial Telegraph Administration. While in the United States, he, with Tsai Ting-kan, was sent to work in the machine shops in Lowell, Massachusetts. Because of the danger of working among the moving machinery, both of the lads were given special permission to cut off their pigtails. Chu Pao-fay, better known to his fellow students in America as "Flounder", was another of the students whom Shen Kung-pao, the Director of the China Merchants Steam Navigation Company, took into his office. He served as Director of the

Shanghai Telegraph office, and later he was appointed Vice Minister of Communications. His failing health forced him to retire from active service before the advent of the republic. He died in Shanghai in 1925.

Chow Wan-pung spent his entire career in the telegraph administration, serving in different capacities until 1909, when he became Director General of the Imperial Telegraph Administration. Yuen Chan-kwon was another who spent most of his career in the telegraph service. He was eventually appointed Chief of the Telegraph section of the Board of Communications. Ching Ta-yeh, upon graduating from the Telegraph College, was sent to Kiatka to establish the telegraph line connecting Peking with Mongolia. Likewise Woo Huan-yung built the first telegraph lines in Kiangsi. Tao Ting-king spent forty-eight years in the Telegraph Administration and ended his career as Director of the Telegraph system in Hupeh province.

Others in the telegraph service either died young or did not reach such prominent positions. There can be little doubt, however, that the twenty or so students of the Educational Mission who built and manned the first lines played an important role in extending the telegraph to the various provinces of China. How much influence they were able to exert in keeping the telegraph lines under the exclusive control of the Chinese Government, it would be difficult to say. The knowledge which they possessed enabled China to embark upon this phase of modern communications without depending on foreign experts, and for this reason the telegraph administration was kept quite free from foreign political interference.

CHAPTER VII

MINES AND RAILWAYS

The Chinese and the Egyptians share credit for first developing mining on a large scale. The early historical records of China show that in remote antiquity the Chinese mined most of the important metals. Anyone who examines the splendid funerary bronzes made by the Shang peoples in the second and first milleniums B.C. will be struck immediately by the tremendous skill in metallurgy which was required to cast these magnificent objects of the smith's craft. The early Chinese were not only masters of the fabrication of objects made of metal, but at a very early date they had developed some mining techniques which in the West were only discovered at a comparatively late date. By means of bamboo drills fastened to the ends of long ropes, they were able to bore salt wells to a depth of several thousand feet and in the T'ang dynasty, the Chinese were already prospecting for deposits by means of core boring or drilling. The records of the Han dynasty, which ruled China from approximately 200 B.C. to 200 A.D., reveal that the use of coal and coke was quite common. Despite these early discoveries, however, mining in agricultural China remained unimportant, but in modern times the advent of the steamship and the steam engine in China gave a great stimulus to the development of China's mineral resources.

After the disastrous wars of 1840 and 1856, leading officials began to memorialize the Throne advocating the exploitation of the large coal and iron resources of the empire as a part of the program to strengthen China in the face of Occidental aggression. Only slight mention was ever made in these memorials of any benefits that might accrue to the masses of Chinese by the development of the nation's natural resources. The whole emphasis was placed upon what the memorialists called the "national restrengthening" of the country.

At first the Imperial Government gave little heed to these pleas. The danger of arousing the population because of the widely spread belief in the *fêng shui* of any given locality had to be taken into consideration and the Court was reluctant to cross the people in this matter. *Fêng shui* was the ancient Chinese belief that the spirits of the dead and the spirits of nature could exercise a considerable influence upon the fortunes of the living. The spirits of nature dwelt in the rocks and hills and rivers, and it was the universally held belief that the ghosts of the dead continued to dwell in the graves for some time after death and could send forth good or evil influences according to whether they were pleased or displeased by the actions of the living. To dig or blast in the earth or to disturb the ancestral graves was a sure way to offend the spirits of nature and to stir up the animosity of the ghosts of the dead. Gradually, however, practical considerations caused the Imperial Government to permit some of the Viceroys and provincial governors to initiate mining and railway enterprises. One of these considerations was the need for a domestic source of coal for the increasing number of steam vessels calling at coastal ports and plying the inland rivers. At first most of the coal used by such vessels had to be imported either from Great Britain or from Australia. In fact, the port of Tientsin owed much of its growth to this early coal trade. Some attempts were made by Chinese merchants to meet the demand for cheap coal by hauling it from the domestic mines to the ports, but the primitive methods of transportation made the domestic coal so expensive that despite the cost of the long haul, it was found that British and Australian coal could be laid down in Chinese ports cheaper than the local product. Nevertheless, coal remained very expensive and the foreign shipowners were eager to secure a cheap domestic supply. The usual diplomatic pressure was brought to bear upon the Imperial Government to open the country to the development of foreign mining activities. The American Minister reminded the Chinese Government, that "the riches which the Creator of all things has deposited in all countries in their soil, are designed by Him for the benefit of mankind." No mining concessions, however, were granted to foreigners and, as in other fields, the initiative in mining enterprises was left up to the Viceroys.

Again it was Li Hung-chang who brooked the superstitions of the people. In 1874 he began to experiment with modern mining machinery in order to work a rich vein of bituminous coal located in western Chihli. This vein had been worked by primitive Chinese methods since early in the 15th century. Li now wanted to develop it in order to have a supply of coal for the numerous ships of the China Merchants Steam Navigation Company. Although it was some two hundred and fifty miles inland, he deliberately chose this location in order to avoid trouble with the coal merchants who supplied Peking with coal from the nearby mines of Mentoku and Chien Tang. The Viceroy told Mr. E. T. Sheperd, the American Consul at Tientsin, that if he attempted to introduce modern machinery into the mines of either of these latter places, he would be sure to meet with serious opposition from the capital, whereas, remote from Peking, the coal merchants would let him alone.

In order to facilitate the transportation of the coal from the mines in western Chihli, he planned to build a horse-drawn tramway from the mines to the Chang Ho river, some thirty miles distant. Possibly the haul was too great to make this project successful, for a few years later Li turned his attention to the development of sources of coal much nearer Tientsin. These were the K'aiping mines at Tongshan, some seventy miles north of Tientsin. Under his auspices, there was formed the K'aiping Mining Company, and in 1878 the exploitation of the Tongshan deposits got under way.

The history of this enterprise is closely bound up with the introduction of Western technology in China. The man who

originally inspired the whole project was Tong King-sing, who it
will be recalled was in the 1840's a classmate of Yung Wing
in the Robert Morrison School in Canton. While Yung Wing
was away at school in America, Tong King-sing had become
one of the China's first modern merchants. When Yung Wing
returned to China in 1854, he and Tong joined forces in advocating the formation of a Chinese steamship company to compete with the foreign concerns and to prevent the coastal and
inland commerce of China from falling entirely into foreign
hands. The result of their enthusiasm was the formation of the
China Merchants Steam Navigation Company, with Tong King-
sing as its managing director. Under his able management the
Company soon acquired a fleet of steam vessels enabling it to
take over a large share of the coastal and river trade from the
British and other foreign operators.

Tong wanted a domestic supply of coal for the vessels of
the China Merchants fleet while Li Hung-chang was equally
interested in finding coal for his ever growing naval squadron.
The result was the formation of the K'aiping Mining Company
to develop the mines.

When the Educational Mission was recalled in 1881, the
K'aiping mines were fairly well developed and a short railroad
had been constructed to haul the coal to a nearby canal for
transportation to Tientsin. This railway was the first railway to
be built in China upon the initiative of the Chinese. It was later
extended to become the Great Peking-Tientsin-Shanhaikuan system connecting Peking with Manchuria. The return of the students gave the directors of the mines the opportunity to establish a school of assaying and mining at Tongshan. Seven of the
returned students were assigned to this school, which was taught
by Mr. E. K. Buttles, an American engineer. The students who
were sent to the Tongshan mining school were Woo Yang-tsang
(Y. T. Woo), Kwong Young-kong, Chun Wing-kwai, Lok
Sik-kwai, Tong Kwo-on, Liang Pao-chew, and Kwong King-

yang. Most of these students eventually played a very active part in the development of modern mining throughout the empire. They were China's first mining engineers and to them was entrusted the development of mines from Manchuria in the east to China's far western province of Kansu.

The K'aiping Mining Company grew to become the largest and most important mining enterprise in all China. Until 1900 it remained entirely in Chinese hands, but after the Boxer episode, foreign interests forced their way into the Company and it became largely controlled by British and American interests. At the same time, most of the engineering and managerial staff continued to be supplied from among the ranks of China's ever growing band of trained engineers and, as in the case of the Imperial Telegraph system, the Chinese Educational Mission students formed the nucleus from which this band grew.

One of the most interesting of the Educational Mission students who were sent to the mining school at Tongshan was Woo Yang-tsang, known in his American school days as "Alligator" and later in life among the foreign community of Tientsin and North China as Y. T. Woo. In 1881 he had passed his entrance examinations and was about to enter Columbia University when the recall of the Mission prevented him from embarking upon his university education. Upon his return to China, he was sent to the Tongshan mines where he stayed until 1886. Fortunately, in that year, through the influence of Li Hung-chang, he was sent to London to the Royal School of Mines, graduating from this institution in 1890 as a fully trained mining engineer. Back in China, he was made engineer-in-chief of some large silver mines in Jehol and, in 1895, he became superintendent of some coal and copper mines near Nanking. In 1897 the Governor of Chekiang province commissioned him to make a survey of the mineral deposits in that province. In 1899 he returned to the K'aiping Mining Company to become Assistant Director and Chief Chemist. During the Boxer troubles of 1900 he was able to render a great service to the Company by keeping the mines out of the hands of the Boxers and also from occupation by Russian troops. When the European staff withdrew to Tientsin, he remained at his post and organized the miners into an armed force to guard the mines against the depredations of the Boxers and other bandits. At the same time, he kept the mines going and was able to supply Tientsin with the much needed coal during the Boxer crisis. The Russians were very anxious to use the disturbed conditions as an excuse to get control of the mining properties and they made several attempts to send troops there to take over the mines. But the volunteer guard under the able leadership of Y. T. Woo prevented the Russians from taking advantage of the situation to seize the mines.

After the K'aiping mining properties passed into the hands of British interests, Y. T. Woo stayed on with the company serving in various important capacities until his retirement in 1920. He died in Peking in 1939. He was one of the first Chinese to spend his whole life in what we in the Occident call a "technical career" and, therefore, he was one of the first Chinese to view Chinese society from the viewpoint of an engineer.

After the Boxer disturbances had quieted down, the K'aiping Mining Company was converted into a British concern, although the Chinese interests retained a great deal of control of the properties. The company now became known as the Chinese Engineering and Mining Company, Limited, and Herbert C. Hoover, then a young engineer, became the first general manager of the new company. Eventually, this concern was amalgamated with the Lan Chow Mining Company, another of Li Hung-chang's enterprises, and thereafter the combined companies were known as the Kailan Mining Administration. The K'aiping mines have remained, to the present, the outstanding coal mining properties in all China. The domination of foreign interests in the company in later years has tended to obscure the fact that the original enterprise came into being and was largely developed through Chinese initiative and with the aid of Chinese engineers such as Woo Yang-tsang, Kwong Young-kong, and others.

Kwong Young-kong was one of the few students of the Mission who upon returning to China were assigned to just the careers they wanted. His father had been a gold miner in Australia and had come home with a modest fortune in gold nuggets. This determined the young boy to become a mining engineer. In 1871, when Yung Wing was searching for boys whose parents would be willing to allow them to go to America for fifteen years, he found a ready response from Kwong Young-kong's family. His uncle was Kwong Chi-chin, a famous dictionary writer and friend of Yung Wing. Through this connection young Kwong was able to go to America in the Educational Mission. He had a distinguished career as a mining engineer and from 1905 until his retirement in 1927 he was Engineer-in-Chief at the Lin Ch'eng collieries in Chihli. In 1909 he was able to render valuable service to the Chinese Government by establishing the valuation of the Pen Hsi-hu coal mines, near Mukden. Through his evaluation, the Chinese and the Japanese interests arrived at an equitable basis of joint participation in this enterprise.

Tong Kwo-on, later known as Tong Kai-son, was another of the Educational Mission students, who became one of the early employees of the K'aiping Mining Company. The son of Tong King-sing, he owed his place in the mission to the early friendship which existed between his father and Yung Wing. Upon his return to China, he became secretary of the Company and right hand man of Chang Yen-mao, the able Chinese director of the Company. Later, Tong Kai-son became the first president of Tsing Hua college. The college was established to train students who were to go to the United States under the arrangements by which the American Government returned to China its share of the Boxer Indemnity. In fact, among the Chinese, Tong Kai-son usually is given the credit for having been the first to suggest that the Boxer Indemnity funds be used to send Chinese students to American universities. Regardless of where the credit lies for the original conception of this scheme, its value to China has been inestimable. Its plan follows closely the original plan of Yung Wing for the Chinese Educational Mission, and it can be said to be a logical successor to the Educational Mission. Under its auspices, thousands of highly selected young Chinese have received the very best technical and liberal educations American universities have to offer.

The story of China's first railways is closely bound up with the development of coal mining in North China. Just as the needs of the China Merchants Steam Navigation Company for a cheap domestic supply of coal gave Tong King-sing the idea of developing the great K'aiping collieries, the need to transport the coal from the mines to the seaboard brought into existence China's first railway. Designed at first to be little more than a horse-drawn tramway, it eventually became the great Peking-Tientsin-Shanhaikuan Railway.

As was true of the telegraph, the first railway to be built upon China's own initiative was preceded by an attempt of some foreigners to force a railway upon China. This was the effort in 1875 of the foreign merchants at Shanghai to build a railway between Shanghai and Woosung, a small village at the mouth of the Yangtze River. The incident is interesting as it again illustrates what took place when the aggressive West collided with the stabilized culture of China. The promoters of the Woosung railway apparently hoped to convert the Chinese to railway transportation by means of a practical demonstration of its utility and cheapness. As Woosung is only twelve miles from Shanghai and the area in between is very thickly populated, it seemed an ideal situation in which to launch this practical demonstration. The scheme was first broached in 1865, but the declared opposition of the native population along the way against anything that might disturb the *fêng shui* of the neighborhood thwarted the promoters from carrying out their plan. They decided to purchase the land along the right of way, ostensibly to construct a horse road between Shanghai and Woosung, but in reality to build the railroad. By 1875 all the necessary land had been purchased but not at the cheap prices which the promoters had first expected. Rumor had got around as to their real aims and the Chinese land owners took advantage of the necessity to acquire the land to boost prices. The land once in hand a railway company was formed and light engines and steel rails were imported from England. Construction on the road proceeded rapidly and on February 14, 1876, sufficient rails had been laid to make a trial run of the "Pioneer," one of the engines that had been imported for the road. This trial run of the "Pioneer" was an important event in the history of China, for this was the first time that a railway train had been operated on Chinese soil.

The Chief Magistrate of Shanghai now notified the Company that it had no authority to construct the railway and that further operations upon it would have to stop immediately. The foreigners simply ignored the protests of the Magistrate and construction proceeded until Woosung was reached. The foreign reports of the affair all agree that once the line was in operation the populace along the way made no effort to disturb it, and that, on the contrary, they showed a great interest in the railway and readily availed themselves of the cheap and convenient form of transportation it offered. The Chinese reports, perhaps equally prejudiced, say that the railway greatly disturbed the calm and quiet of the people and that it was only with difficulty that they were prevented from forcibly removing it. After the line had been in operation for a few months, a Chinese who was walking along the tracks was killed either accidentally by an oncoming train or by throwing himself under it. Whatever had been the true temper of the people up to this time, there was no mistaking their attitude after this unfortunate accident. They became exceedingly hostile and made further operation of the road impossible. The Chinese authorities now stepped in and purchased the line, presumably with the intention of operating it under government control. However, when in October 1877, the last installment of the purchase price was paid to the Company, the rails were removed and the engines and rolling stock were conveyed to Formosa.

From an Occidental viewpoint the action of the Chinese officials in removing the railway seems narrow and unreasonable. But in constructing the railway without the express permission of the Chinese Government and, in fact, over the protests of the local magistrate, the Chinese element of "face" became involved. The magistrate, and back of him, the Governor and Viceroy of the province either had to remove the railway or allow the foreigners openly to flout their authority. In the latter case a considerable loss of prestige or "face" would ensue. Furthermore, the leading Chinese officials were united in their determination that no railways should be built in China unless they remained under Chinese control. The Chinese were not, eventually, to sustain this policy, but they did cling to it as long as possible.

Western writers have also made much of the fact that the rolling stock and rails of the Woosung railway were dumped on the beach at Formosa where they were allowed to rust away. This is true, but that was not the intention when the materials were first sent there. They were intended for the use of the Governor of Formosa, who had long been memorializing the Throne to permit him to construct a railway in Formosa, both in order to defend it better from Japanese aggression and to overcome the lack of roads in the island. Political changes prevented him from using the Woosung rails and engines, but the original intention had been to use them there.

The history of the K'aiping railway is much more pleasant to follow. It was a Chinese line from the beginning and, except for a few foreign employees, foreigners were excluded from participation in the development of the railway, at least in its early stages. Tong King-sing, the head of the China Merchants Steam Navigation Company, working with the approbation and support of Li Hung-chang, constructed this railway as a means of getting the coal from the mines at K'aiping down to the docks at Taku Bar, near Tientsin. The nearest shipping point to the collieries was on the Pehtang River, some twenty-nine miles from the mines. At first the K'aiping Mining Company, through the aid of Li Hung-chang, sought permission to construct a tramway between Tongshan and the Pehtang. In due course Imperial permission was received and construction was about to begin when suddenly the Imperial sanction was withdrawn. The reversal was caused by the intense political rivalry that existed between Li Hung-chang and Chang Chih-tung, the other great reforming Viceroy of the time. Chang protested against construction of the road on the grounds that it would open the capital to invasion by foreign troops, but his real object seems to have been to strike at Li Hung-chang. The Court was also influenced by the pleas of the many boatmen and other people who gained their livelihood in transporting goods along the canals to the capital. As they feared that the construction of the railway would menace their livelihood, they brought pressure to have the plan quashed.

Attempts were now made to construct a canal connecting the collieries with the Pehtang River, but when it proved impossible to bring the canal to the mines, Imperial sanction was procured to construct a tramway from the mines to the head of the canal, some seven miles away. Both Tong King-sing and Mr. C. W. Kinder, the Chief Engineer, were determined that this short line should be constructed upon a standard gauge, as they believed that in time permission would be given to use engines in place of mules to draw the coal trucks and also that the line would be eventually extended to Tientsin. In spite of opposition by the shareholders of the Company who objected to the increased cost, the line was constructed on a standard gauge.

So confident was Mr. Kinder of the eventual use of locomotives on the line that he began to build a small engine from whatever materials he had at hand. When the Court learned of his efforts he was forbidden to complete the engine, but he persisted, and on June 9, 1881, his engine was christened the "Rocket of China". It was put into immediate use and soon other locomotives and cars were purchased. Almost unnoticed, China's first railway thus came into being. In 1882 the line was extended to Lutai, the nearest point on the Pehtang River. When this section was completed, Li Hung-chang adroitly addressed the Throne through the Board of Admiralty and secured permission to extend the line at both ends, northwards to Shanhaikuan and southward to Tientsin. No mention was made in the Admiralty's memorial to the Throne of the commercial advantages of such extensions but a great deal was made of how they would greatly increase the efficiency of defending the coast. It was on this basis that Imperial sanction was secured. The section to Tientsin was completed in August, 1887, and thereafter the line was gradually extended until it finally formed a complete link between Peking, Tientsin, and Shanhaikuan, on the Sino-Manchurian border. Li Hung-chang planned to connect this line with a vast system of railways which would have embraced all Manchuria, but the Sino-Japanese war of 1895 postponed this project until the 1920's.

Foreigners, in the hope of gaining the support of the Court, made several ludicrous attempts to interest the Empress Dowager in railroads by presenting to the Court miniature locomotives and fancifully decorated coaches. In 1874 certain British interests offered to the Emperor Tung Chih a small railway completely equipped in every detail, but this offer was

104

politely refused. In 1889 a French Syndicate presented to Prince Chun six railway carriages built in France and displaying every skill and artifice of French railway construction. Three of the carriages were fitted in yellow, green, and blue satin with all the necessary sleeping and toilet arrangements. No locomotives were sent with the carriages, as it was intended that they should be used within the Imperial City and should be drawn by eunuchs over a small line to be laid down there. The Syndicate hoped that by this means the Court would come to realize the comforts and ease of travelling by railroad and would be thus won over to an extensive use of railway transportation in China.

Mr. M. T. Liang, one of the former students of the Educational Mission, tells an amusing story about the problem of unloading these cars from the ship which brought them to Tientsin and of the difficulty he experienced in getting them up to Peking. At the time the cars arrived there were no cranes or mechanical unloading facilities at the docks of Tientsin, and the French engineer who had been sent in charge of the cars was much concerned as to how they would be lifted from the hold of the ship and placed on barges. Mr. Liang assured him that a gang of Chinese coolies working under the direction of an experienced foreman would have no trouble in rigging up a tackle which would enable them to unload the heavy cars. He then persuaded the somewhat worried Frenchman to go home with him for the night. The next morning when they returned, the cars had already been unloaded and reposed on barges awaiting their transportation up the Pei Ho river to Tungchow. Getting the cars from Tungchow to Peking, a distance of some twelve miles, also presented a problem, but this was solved with the aid of an army of coolies and numerous long poles. The poles were laid down to form a series of rollers over which the coolies pulled the cars, and they were thus transported to Peking without incident. The actual moving of the cars was done at night in order to cause the least excitement possible among the villages through which the procession had to pass. The Empress Dowager and her ladies no doubt enjoyed riding on these cars, but their presence in the Imperial City seems to have had not the slightest effect in bringing her to a more favorable frame of mind with regard to the introduction of railways into China.

Another attempt to convince by ocular demonstration was made by some American concessionaire hunters who, around 1885, sent to the Imperial Court a complete working model railway. It consisted of a thousand feet of main track and sideings, with switches, turntable, a passenger locomotive and tender, mail and baggage cars, Pullman parlor and sleeping cars, different kinds of freight cars, and a full section of seats and berths. The cars were five feet long and all other parts of the model were in proportion. Great care had been taken to make the model an exact miniature of railway cars in actual use in the United States. The model was first presented to Li Hung-chang, who, in turn, presented it to Prince Chun, the father of the Emperor. It was set up in the Imperial Palace grounds in Peking where the Emperor and Empress Dowager seemed to be greatly intrigued by it.

No doubt such devices did materially assist reformers such as Li Hung-chang in winning the support of the Court for their various schemes to introduce railways into China, but they did not aid the concessionaires in their pursuit of profitable contracts from the Chinese Government. China became a happy hunting ground for the concessionaire only after the events of 1898, when, led by Germany, the Europeans abandoned persuasion in favor of force in pressing upon China the fruits of Western civilization. Because of military pressure on every side, the Chinese statesmen gave up as hopeless their fight to keep the foreigner from gaining control of China's natural resources and the arteries of inland commerce. The policy of refusing to permit foreigners to develop mines, telegraphs, and railways, a policy successfully maintained for over forty years, now gave way to the wholesale granting of concessions in the hope that those made to the nationals of one nation would serve to check rights granted to the nationals of a rival power. The powers countered this with the attempt to carve China into a series of mutually exclusive spheres of interest. It was this situation which gave rise to the famous "Open Door" policy of the United States and Great Britain. To a certain degree, the "Open Door" policy staved off what was generally looked forward to as "the break-up of China".

When the students of the Mission first returned to China, there seemed little prospect that the Imperial Government would ever consent to the construction of any extensive system of railways in the empire. In the minds of Chinese officials railways embodied a much greater threat to the independence of China than did any of the other technical devices of the foreigners. There seems to have been a widespread fear that railways would only serve as means whereby foreign armies could quickly penetrate into the interior. The Chinese felt confident of preserving their way of life and the integrity of the empire as long as the foreigner was confined to the coast, but once he were permitted to gain an easy access to the interior, they felt that all would soon be lost.

Perhaps this attitude explains why Li Hung-chang failed to establish a railway school similar to the telegraph and naval schools he founded at Tientsin. The result was that no systematic effort was made to train any of the returned students from the Educational Mission in the art of railway building and operation. Yet this field of activity proved to be one in which they demonstrated in a very marked degree their usefulness to the new China. Most of the students who became identified with the early railroads of China turned to railroading as a career after having spent some time as engineers in the navy or in other governmental capacities. The chief characteristics which gained the "American boys" ultimate recognition was the fact that they could get things done and, in the field of railway construction where efficient action was necessary, they slowly gained the recognition which they deserved. Such was the case, for instance, of Liang Yu-ho, better known in foreign circles as M. T. Liang, and of Jeme Tien-yow. The latter will always be remembered by the Chinese as being the first engineer to construct an important railway entirely independent of foreign aid.

Liang Yu-ho, or M. T. Liang, secured a place in the Chinese Educational Mission through the influence of his uncle, who was a prosperous merchant in Shanghai. In the United States, he was educated at the grammar school in Springfield, Massachusetts, and at the Hartford High School. When, in 1881, the Mission was recalled, he had spent a year or so at the Stevens School of Technology. Upon his return to China, he was sent as a draftsman to the West Arsenal at Tientsin. In 1883 he was one of the returned students who were ordered by Li Hung-chang to accompany Mr. Von Mollendorf to Korea to establish the Korean Customs Service. Later, when Yüan Shih-k'ai become the Chinese Resident at the Korean Court and the direction of Korean affairs fell into his hands, M. T. Liang and the others who were in Korea with him rose to very high positions in the Korean service. He stayed in Korea until 1894, returning to China at the time Yüan Shih-k'ai was recalled from Korea. Upon his return he entered the service of the Peking-Shanhaikuan Railway as Superintendent of the Traffic Department. During the course of the Boxer troubles, the railway was seized by the allied armies and was kept under military control until September 29, 1902, when suddenly, upon twenty-four hours' notice, it was handed back to the Chinese. The Chinese authorities were somewhat discomfited by this unexpected turn of affairs and turned to M. T. Liang to aid them. He assumed charge of the railway and carried on its functioning without any interruption. His record as manager was most brilliant. When the railway was first turned back to Chinese control, the Chinese Government was subsidizing it with $1,500 000 Mex. per year, but when M. T. Liang, relinquished its management some years later, the railway was earning about a million taels (approx. $300,000 Mex.) per month. He attained this remarkable record by initiating such schemes as transporting the coolies to Manchuria for the annual harvests at the extremely low fare of $2.50 Mex. ($1.50, U.S.) per head. About 400,000 coolies went from North China to Manchuria each year, and, until M. T. Liang devised this low fare, they walked overland. By going by rail they saved at least one month's time and consequently increased the amount of money they were able to bring back with them.

As manager of the railway, M. T. Liang occupied an official rank far below that of the Tientsin Magistrate, but whereas the Taotai received about $140 Mex. per month salary, M. T. Liang was paid the handsome salary of $2000 Mex. per month. Prejudice was still too strong to grant these "westerners" the official rank they deserved, but, by now, their value was at least reckoned in a financial way. This was a very different state of affairs from that which prevailed when they first returned, when they were paid the paltry sum of five taels per month, or little more than a government office clerk or yamen messenger received.

Another venture in which M. T. Liang demonstrated his ability to get things done was the building of the branch line from the Peking-Tientsin Railway to the Western Masolea where the Ch'ing emperors and their consorts were buried. Each Spring the Court made the journey of some twenty-seven miles to the tombs in order to pay their respect to the Imperial ancestors. In the late Autumn of 1906 the Empress Dowager conceived the idea of having a railway built to the tombs in order to save the court from the fatigue of the journey by cart and palanquin. The railway was to be completed by the following March. Foreign engineers were unwilling to attempt to construct the railway in such a short time, but M. T. Liang volunteered to undertake the task. He enlisted the aid of Jeme Tien-yau another Educational Mission student, and they completed it in time for the annual Court pilgrimage.

Not all of M. T. Liang's ventures, however, were as successful as was his management of the railway. In his enthusiasm for western transportation, he persuaded the Empress Dowager to permit him to import a fleet of auto busses to carry the Court back and forth between the Winter Palace in Peking and the Summer Palace some eight miles out in the country. Unfortunately, the busses scared the horses of the officials and after several of them had been unceremoniously dumped into the muddy ditches along the way, the busses were ordered removed. They eventually were sent to Kalgan, where they rendered many years of service in transporting officials and travellers across the desert roads of Mongolia.

At the end of the Russo-Japanese war, the abilities of such men as M. T. Liang could no longer be overlooked nor could they be confined to purely non-political positions. In 1906, Liang was appointed Commissioner of Customs at Newchang, the most important port in Manchuria, and a post, heretofore, always reserved for a Manchu of high rank. Liang was appointed primarily to negotiate with the Japanese the retrocession of the Liaotung Peninsula, which the latter had occupied during the course of the Russo-Japanese war. He succeeded admirably in this difficult negotiation and was able to whittle the Japanese leasehold down to the southernmost tip of the peninsula. From Newchang he was transferred to Tientsin, where he was in charge of the customs. From Tientsin he went to the very lucrative and attractive post of Customs intendant of Shanghai. This post was considered to be better than most viceroyalties and one greatly coveted in the Chinese official world. He received the appointment because the Court considered him the only official who could persuade the foreign Municipal Council at Shanghai to cooperate in the suppression of the Opium traffic within the

International Concession. He persuaded the Shanghai Council to take vigorous measures against the Opium traffic and thus to rid China of one of its chief sources of the supply of the drug.

From Shanghai he was sent to Manchuria to become Governor of Fêngtien Province. Later, under the Republic, he became Minister of Foreign Affairs. In 1921 he served as High Adviser to the Chinese Delegation to the Washington Conference. His last service to China was to negotiate with the British Government for the return of the concession at Weihaiwei. He died in Tientsin on October 14, 1941.

M. T. Liang's career well illustrates the gradual change in the attitude of the Chinese Government towards the Chinese Educational Mission students. When they first returned to China, they were considered mere mechanics, deserving only slightly better treatment than that accorded to coolies. Gradually their training and their innate strength of character brought them to the fore. After the Boxer disaster of 1900, they began to be valued at their true worth and to receive recognition in accordance with the merit of their achievements.

Associated with M. T. Liang in the building of the short extension line from Fêngtai to the Western Tombs was another former Educational Mission student. This was Jeme Tien-yau, honored by all Chinese as China's first railway builder. It was his work in connection with building the line to the Ch'ing tombs that brought him to the notice of the Imperial Government and gave him the opportunity to build the Peking-Kalgan Railway. Like the majority of the Educational Mission students, he was a Cantonese. He went to America in 1872, with the first contingent of students of the Mission. He was then twelve years of age and exceedingly intelligent and alert. He completed grammar and high school and in 1877 entered the Sheffield School of Engineering at Yale College. He was graduated with honors in 1881, having won the class prize in mathematics in his Freshman and Junior years. Upon his return to China in

1881, he was assigned to the naval school at the Foochow Arsenal. In 1884 he was appointed teacher of naval engineering at the Whampao Naval College in Canton. He remained here until 1888, and thereafter he spent his life as Resident Engineer, Consulting Engineer, and Manager and Director of the various Chinese Government railways. His great achievement, however, was the planning and construction of the railroad between Peking and Kalgan in Mongolia. Because of the extreme height of the mountain passes northwest of Peking, the construction of this railway demanded engineering skill of the highest order. Jeme Tien-yau proved equal to the task imposed upon him and the railway stands today as a fitting memorial to China's first and foremost engineer.

The opportunity for China to build the Peking-Kalgan railway entirely free of foreign aid and interference came about through the machinations of international politics. When the line was first proposed, British interests claimed a prior right to construct it on the grounds that the loan which the British banks had made to the Imperial Government to extend the railway between Peking and Shanhaikuan to Mukden gave it the first opportunity to construct new railways within the Great Wall. Russian interests now came forward and asserted their right to build the railway, claiming that it came within their sphere of interests as its terminus was outside the Great Wall. The Japanese Government, through its minister in Peking, also demanded the right to build the railway as Japan asserted that the Russian rights in this area had reverted to Japan because of her victory over Russia in the Russo-Japanese war of 1905. Faced with the dilemma brought about by these conflicting demands, the Chinese Government now turned to Jeme Tien-yau to survey the line and make an estimate of its cost. On the grounds that the matter was of such an unimportant nature that foreigners would hardly care to bother with it, the work was then entrusted to Jeme Tien-yau, who successfully constructed the line. The completion of this railroad, coming as it did in the midst of an ever rising resentment among the Chinese people at the violations of Chinese sovereignty by foreign interests, was hailed as a national achievement, and Jeme Tien-yau became a national hero. He had the unique distinction of being the first engineer in modern China to attain a nation wide reputation. During the Boxer troubles of 1900 he and Kwong Young-kong, another of the ex-students, nearly lost their lives at the hands of unruly Russian troops. The Russians wanted to force them to operate the railway between the Tongshan mine and Tientsin and threatened to kill them if they did not comply. However, through the cool behavior of Y. T. Woo, who had been left in charge of the mines, they were able to escape. Captain Baldwin, an American who happened to be at the mines, hid them under some bedding in his cart and smuggled them past the Russian guards. Y. T. Woo stayed behind to guard the mines, although he was in constant danger of his life. At one time, in his attempt to defend the mining properties, he was slashed over the face with a riding whip by a Russian general.

Another of the former American students who distinguished himself both in the diplomatic and railway services was Chung Mun-yew. While at Yale College, between 1879 and 1881, he became famous as "Munny," the lightest coxswain the Yale crew ever had had. He was probably the only Chinese who has had the pleasure of materially assisting Yale to victory over Harvard in the annual boat races. Upon his return to China he served for some years as Interpreter in the office of the Shanghai Customs Intendant, but, in 1903, he left this post to become Secretary and Interpreter to the Chinese Legation at Washington. After ten years in Washington, he was sent to Madrid to become Charge d'Affaires. From here he went to Manila as Consul General. In 1906 he entered the Imperial Railway Administration and supervised the construction of the Shanghai-Nanking Railway. Upon its completion, he became

Managing Director of the line. In 1916 he resigned active management of the line to become Commissioner of the Railway. In 1927 he retired from this post and is now living in Shanghai.

Other students of the Mission who served in important positions in the Imperial Railway administration were Wong Chung-liang, successively Managing Director of the Shanghai-Nanking Railway, Vice-President of the Canton-Hankow Railway, and Managing Director of the Tientsin-Pukow Railway; Low Kwock-sui, who surveyed and built lines in Hupei, Kweichow, Yunnan, and Canton; Shen Ke-shu, who for many years served as Paymaster on the Peking-Mukden Railway; Lin Pay-chuan, who was Chief of the Traffic Department of the Peking-Mukden Railway; Tong Chi-yao, who served for many years in the same railway; and Chow Chuen-kan, who was right-hand man and interpreter for C. W. Kinder, the Engineer-in-Chief of the Peking-Mukden line.

In this vital field of the westernization of China, the Educational Mission students played a most important, although very often not conspicuous, part. The tendency still was to grant them only the lower official ranks, but their technical training and their knowledge of the West became increasingly in demand. They could no longer be kept out of positions of trust and importance by the jealously of the mandarins. Many of these mandarins, while occupying the titular positions at the head of the railway, telegraph, mining, and other technical enterprises upon which the Chinese Government embarked, depended upon these first western trained enginers to do the actual construction and management of these governmental projects.

CHAPTER VIII

UP THE MANDARIN'S NINE-RUNG LADDER

In old Imperial China the only road to fame led up through the nine official ranks of the scholar bureaucracy. It was this scholar bureaucracy drawn from the Confucian literati which administered the empire. In general, within China's vast administrative system promotion was slow and depended much more upon seniority than upon ability. Yet occasionally sheer force of character or ability so marked that it could not be overlooked brought rapid promotion to a fortunate official and gained for him the coveted peacock feather or the yellow riding jacket which constituted the highest rewards of Imperial favor. Li Hung-chang was such a one to whom the favorable juxtaposition of time and circumstance and great ability brought highest rank and extraordinary marks of gratitude from the Court. But outside of the few exceptional ones, such as Li Hung-chang and Tsêng Kuo-fan, success in official life depended in a very great measure upon the fortunes which attended the career of the great mandarin to whom an aspiring young official attached himself. Imperial favor extended to the mandarin embraced his subordinates. Imperial disgrace brought with it degradation and loss of rank to mentor and protege alike. Nothing could illustrate this point better than the marked success which attended the careers of some of the students of the Educational Mission who, shortly after their return to China, had the good fortune to be placed in the entourage of Yüan Shih-k'ai. In 1881 Yüan Shih-k'ai was still a young official but already he was looked upon as the logical inheritor of the power and prestige of Viceroy Li Hung-chang. As he climbed the ladder of official preferment he raised with him his subordinates who had loyally served him when he still was on the lower rungs. A mere recital of the names of those who served under

Yüan Shih-k'ai is sufficient to indicate what good fortune attended their association with him, for they represent the most famous of the Educational Mission students and they were the ones who finally achieved national reputations. They were Liang Yu-ho (M. T. Liang), whose work in connection with the Peking-Tientsin-Shanhaikuan Railway has already been mentioned; Tsai Shou-kee, noted for his able administration of the Chinese city of Tientsin and also as founder of the Peiyang University at Tientsin; Tong Shao-yi, the first Prime Minister of the Chinese Republic when it was organized in 1911, and the most famous of all the Educational Mission boys; Woo Chung-yen, who ably represented his country in diplomatic posts throughout the world; Lin Pay-chuan, closely associated with the development of the great Peking-Mukden Railway system; and lastly Chow Chang-ling, much better known as Sir Shouson Chow, for many years the representative of the large Chinese population in the British colony of Hong Kong.

The association of these men with Yüan Shih-k'ai came about through sheer luck rather than through any marked foresight on their part. In 1881 Li Hung-chang embarked upon a forward policy in Korea. The aim of this policy was to bring Korea back into the Imperial fold from which she was in danger of being enticed by the blandishments of Russia and Japan. Li opened his campaign by sending to Korea Baron P. C. Von Mollendorf. Mollendorf's job was to reorganize the Korean Customs along the lines of the Chinese Imperial Maritime Customs. To assist Von Mollendorf in this task, Li Hung-chang sent along with him a group of young Chinese, among whom were the six former students of the Educational Mission mentioned above.

Von Mollendorf's work in Korea was crowned with success and in a very short time the Korean Customs service was brought under the direction of the Imperial Chinese Customs. In furtherance of the policy of asserting China's hegemony in

Korea, Li Hung-chang in 1884 sent Yüan Shih-k'ai to Korea to be the Chinese Resident at Seoul, the capital of Korea.

Li Hung-chang's forward policy in Korea was temporarily successful, but in the long run it was bound to bring to a head the conflicting ambitions of China and Japan. Between 1884 and 1894 Yüan became the virtual ruler of Korea but his domination of Korean affairs only served to increase the uneasiness of Japan. In 1894 the Japanese decided to act and there ensued the Sino-Japanese war over Korea. Yüan was hurriedly recalled but his failure seems not to have checked his career, for soon after his return the Empress Dowager showed her trust in him by raising him to higher and higher honors. Naturally this gave him ample opportunity to bring to the favorable notice of the Court the qualities of his subordinates. The consequence was that such men as Tong Shao-yi and Liang Yu-ho advanced rapidly up the ladder of official rank and power. All this came to an end in 1915 when Yüan, unable to restrain his over-weening ambition, plotted to overthrow the republic and to establish a new dynasty. When this plot failed, his followers also fell into disgrace, but by this time his former subordinates in Korea had achieved such marked positions of honor that in their cases disgrace meant little more than a well-earned retirement from official life.

In Tong Shao-yi we again see how remarkable were the influences upon the modernization of China which flowed from the small band of Chinese youths who in the 1840's formed the first class to be taught in the Morrison Educational Society School at Canton. Tong Shao-yi was the nephew of Tong King-sing, schoolmate of Yung Wing and founder of the China Merchants Steam Navigation Company. This Company was China's first commercial steamship line and was also China's first stock company. Tong King-sing was also the moving spirit in the development of the K'aiping coal mines in North China. In turn the development of these mines gave rise to the construction of China's first railway, the little tramway between the K'aiping mines and the Lutai canal. It was through his remarkable uncle that Tong Shao-yi was able to take a place in the third detachment of students who left for the United States in 1874. In the United States his intellectual brilliance soon marked him as one of the most gifted of the Mission students. Graduated with honors from Hartford High School in 1880, he entered Columbia University but, as was true of most of the other students, his university education was cut short by the recall of the Mission in the summer of 1881. Upon his return to China he was sent to Korea with Von Mollendorf, but when in 1884 Yüan Shih-k'ai arrived in Seoul as Chinese Resident, he selected Tong Shao-yi to be his confidential secretary. Tong narrowly escaped assassination in the troubles of that year when several high Korean officials were murdered as an incident in the fierce diplomatic struggle between China and Japan for control of the kingdom. Von Mollendorf rescued Tong Shao-yi and hid him in his house until order had been restored. It is impossible to trace the actual influence of Tong Shao-yi upon the course of affairs in Korea at this time and especially upon the maintenance of Chinese influence in the face of determined Russian and Japanese pressure to oust China from Korea. Tong Shao-yi was still a very young man and although his position as secretary of the great Yüan Shih-k'ai must have given him unparalled opportunities to exercise a decided influence upon Korean affairs, it was his chief who took the praise and blame for executing whatever suggestions Tong Shao-yi might have made.

After 1900, however, Tong's career becomes easier to follow. In the last decade of its existence the rapidly weakening Manchu dynasty again and again called upon him to manage the many difficult situations which arose between China and foreign nations. He first won a wide reputation for great capability during the Boxer troubles of 1900. At this time he was the Chief Magistrate of the Chinese section of the city of Tientsin and as such he acted as an intermediary between the foreign authorities and the Chinese. After 1900 Tientsin was governed by an allied military commission but such was the high regard in which Tong was held by the foreign community that in 1902 the control of the city was returned to him. The position of Taotai or Chief Magistrate at Tientsin was a very lucrative one and offered many opportunities for personal enrichment, but Tong was so honest that he achieved the almost unique distinction among Chinese officials of leaving his post at the end of three years as poor as when he took office.

In 1904 he was called upon to deal with another difficult situation. This was to go to Tibet as Special Representative of the Imperial Government in order to arrange a settlement with the British authorities of the long standing and difficult problem of the Tibeto-Indian border. While carrying out this task he became friends with Lord Kitchener, who was the representative of Great Britain in the negotiations.

In 1906, his mission to Tibet having been brought to a successful conclusion, Tong returned to Peking to become Vice-President in the Ministry of Foreign Affairs. In the following year he was appointed to a similar post in the Ministry of Communications. All these positions were preparations for his really important services to China, which began with his appointment as Governor General of Fêngtien province in Manchuria. This was a most signal honor as Fêngtien was the ancestral home of the Manchu Imperial family and heretofore only a Manchu of the highest rank had held this post. Tong owed his appointment to Yüan Shih-k'ai, who at this time was all powerful in Peking. Yüan wanted Tong to counteract the aggressions of the Japanese and Russians in Manchuria, where both nations made no secret of their design to divide Manchuria between them.

In Manchuria Tong soon became fast friends with Willard Straight, the American "Cecil Rhodes" of the Far East. Straight spoke of Tong as "one of the cleverest men in China." Although

119

only a very young man at this time, Willard Straight was not without his own claim to fame. He was a young American of excellent education and from a family of some means. As American Consul at Mukden he had become fascinated by the great role which he conceived the United States could play in the industrial development of China. He was that curious combination of an idealist and an extremely practical business man. His idea was to preserve Chinese sovereignty but at the same time to make American participation in the development of China's natural resources pay high dividends to the American investor. In 1908 he held the modest post of American Consul at Mukden but he used his position as a listening post from which to sound out the Chinese on his vast schemes of Sino-American cooperation in the industrial and railway development of Manchuria. These schemes, which Straight conceived in the best Cecil Rhodes tradition, envisioned the use of the financial resources of the United States to develop the rich natural resources of Manchuria. In his mind, American participation in no way implied the weakening of Chinese sovereignty. In fact, he believed the opposite to be true, for he felt that only through Sino-American cooperation would China be able to ward off the disintegration which threatened the empire through the rapaciousness of Japan and the European powers.

In Tong Shao-yi, Straight found just the Chinese statesman he needed for the realization of his schemes. Not only could Tong talk "American," but he had arrived at the same conclusion; namely, that unless one or more of the politically disinterested powers could be opposed to Russia and Japan, Manchuria would soon be lost to China. During the course of 1908 Tong and Straight perfected their ideas for a large currency reform and industrial development loan for Manchuria and for the projection of a series of American-financed, but Chinese-owned, railways designed to check the Japanese and Russian systems.

Meanwhile in Peking, the Imperial Government was faced with mounting difficulties from the various threats to Chinese sovereignty arising from the demands of the powers. France, Russia, and Japan, in particular, seemed to be determined to wring every concession possible from a weak China. Great Britain, although viewing the Chinese scene from the much wider viewpoint of her vast Imperial interests, was none the less not far behind the other powers in her own demands. Germany and the United States remained the only powers politically aloof, and Germany, despite the protestations of friendship on the part of the Kaiser, was suspected by the Chinese. The Chinese could not forget that Germany had opened the "battle for concessions" in 1898 by seizing the port of Kiaochow on the Shantung coast. Now Germany, faced by isolation in the Far East as a result of the Anglo-Japanese alliance and the entente in Europe between Great Britain, France, and Russia, was eager to find support. In fact, the Kaiser had openly proposed an alliance between the United States, Germany, and China in order to preserve the "Open Door."

The Kaiser's idea was now taken up by the Chinese Government and Tong Shao-yi was selected to sound out Germany and the United States on the subject of an understanding among the three nations. Perhaps Tong owed this appointment to the influence of Willard Straight. Straight had already planned a great American loan to China for the development of Manchuria and one of Tong's tasks was to broach this project to the American government.

In July, 1908, Tong was appointed Special Ambassador to Washington, ostensibly to thank the United States for offering to remit further Boxer indemnity funds. His real mission, which was kept very secret, was a threefold one. First, he was to get the promise of Germany and the United States to uphold a declaration upon the part of the Chinese Government of its intention to preserve its territorial integrity and at the same time to follow the principle of the Open Door in all of its international relations. Secondly, in order to counter Russian and Japanese aggression in Manchuria, he was to request the German government to assist in the reorganization of the Chinese army through the loan of numerous military advisers. Finally, he was to invite the American Government to persuade American banking interests to take the lead in financing the economic and railway development of Manchuria. Thus, it was hoped, Japanese and Russian encroachments in Manchuria would be successfully checked.

When Tong left China for the United States, the prospects for the success of his mission were bright. Straight had enlisted the support of the great American financier and railway magnate, E. H. Harriman, and the Kaiser had already indicated his favorable attitude towards some sort of Chinese alliance which would relieve Germany of her increasingly isolated position in the Far East.

As Tong crossed the Pacific towards the shores of America, it must have seemed to him that the task which had been entrusted to him was the fitting culmination of the dreams of Yung Wing and his Educational Mission to the United States of some thirty-five years before. In 1873 Tong had crossed the Pacific as a young lad of thirteen years of age. Now, he was the Special Envoy of the Chinese Emperor and entrusted with a mission, the success of which could bring untold benefits to his country and to his people. How bitter then must have been his chagrin and disappointment when upon the very day he arrived in Washington he found that President Theodore Roosevelt and his Secretary of State, Mr. Elihu Root, had completed all the details and were ready to sign an accord with Japan which seemed to give Japan a free hand in Manchuria. Mr. Root attempted to explain to Tong Shao-yi that the Root-Takahira accord in no way lessened American concern for the territorial integrity of China. Tong, and most of his countrymen with him, believed, however, that Roosevelt in his anxiety to avoid trouble with Japan had deliberately sacrificed China and practically invited Japan to go ahead in Manchuria. Willard Straight, who had hoped that Tong's mission would result in American leadership in the "westernization" of China, was equally disappointed. He believed that Roosevelt had committed a great political blunder which some day would be greatly regretted.

The effect of the Japanese-American accord of 1908 was to create in China a deep distrust of the United States. Its more immediate effect was to cause the downfall of Yüan Shih-k'ai and his dismissal from office. While Tong was in the United States, both the Empress Dowager and the Emperor Kuang Hsü died. Yüan now suffered the heritage of hate which he had incurred at the time of Kuang Hsü's Hundred Days Reforms. It was generally believed that he had been the cause of the failure of that movement and had instigated the subsequent imprisonment of the Emperor by the Empress Dowager. Now that the Empress Dowager could no longer protect Yüan from his enemies, they forced him from office.

With the dismissal and disgrace of Yüan Shih-k'ai his proteges suffered eclipse. Upon Tong Shao-yi's return to China, he gave up all his offices and retired to Tientsin, where he lived surrounded by a host of retainers and poor relations. The revolution of 1911 was to bring both him and Yüan Shih-k'ai back to the forefront of public life. But for several years both of them passed from the political stage.

The downfall of Yüan Shih-k'ai brought to the head of the Imperial Government Chang Chih-tung, the great political rival of Li Hung-chang. Chang, it will be remembered, was one of the great reforming viceroys of the latter part of the nineteenth century. He was not so steadfast in his advocacy of reforms as was Li Hung-chang, yet he was responsible for the development of the great Han-Yeh-p'ing Iron and Steel works at Hankow and for numerous other industrial enterprises. Just as Tong Shao-yi had attached himself to the entourage of Yüan Shih-k'ai, another of the Educational Mission students became the protege of Chang Chih-tung. This was Liang Tun-yen. We shall see that Liang, like Tong Shao-yi, was called upon to serve as a buffer between the old Imperial world of China and the aggressiveness of the new industrial West.

When Liang Tun-yen came to the United States in 1872 with the first detachment of the Chinese Educational Mission, he was fifteen years of age. Upon his arrival he had the good fortune to be one of the boys who went to live with the Bartlett family in Hartford. He attended the West Middle Grammar School and later the Hartford High School. In 1878, he entered Yale University, but was recalled just before the time he would have been graduated. In high school and college he was famous as a baseball player. He was the great south-paw of the "Orientals," the baseball team formed by the boys of the Educational Mission. His erratic delivery became the terror of local teams, especially since it was accomplished by "the most surprising contortions of the body while his cue was describing a series of mathematical curves in the air."

When he first returned to China, he served as a teacher in the Telegraph School at Tientsin, but, in 1884, Chang Chih-tung, who like Li Hung-chang was always on the lookout for bright young men for his entourage, took him into his service. At this time Chang was Viceroy of the Liang Kuang, the two southern provinces of Kuangtung and Kuangsi. In 1886 Liang went to Wuch'ang with Chang Chih-tung, when the latter was transferred to the viceroyalty of the Liang Hu, comprising the Yangtze provinces of Hupei and Hunan. His first claim to fame came in 1900 during the Boxer troubles. At this time he was Secretary and Adviser to Chang Chih-tung and it was his influence which greatly aided Chang in keeping the Liang Hu free of Boxer uprisings and safeguarding the lives and properties of the foreigners in this region.

Liang Yu-ho and Tong Shao-yi in 1872 just prior to leaving for the United States.

Chinese Educational Mission students during their Hartford days. Top, left to right: Yung Leang, naval officer; Chow Chua-chien, railway and mining engineer. Lower: Tsao Kuei-cheong, died in the United States; Wong Kai Kah, diplomat.

Yung Wing as a student at Yale College, 1854.

Mrs. Fannie Bartlett   Professor David Bartlett

Some of the Chinese Educational Mission students during their Hartford days. Top, left to right: Woo Yang-tsang, mining engineer; Kwong Wing-chung, naval officer killed at the battle of Pagoda Anchorage, 1884. Lower, left to right: unidentified; Woo King-yung, naval officer.

Another group of Chinese Educational Mission students during their stay in the United States. Top, left to right: Liang Tun-yen, statesman; Chin Mon-fay, Consular Service. Lower, left to right; Woo Chung-yen, Consular Service; Tong Ching-yao, career unknown.

Some of the students as they landed in San Francisco in 1872.

A reunion of the students in China, Christmas, 1890. Seated, left to right: Liang Pao-chew, Dr. Li Lai-tong, Kwong King-yang (engineer), Tong Sze-chung, and Mr. Yen. Standing, left to right: Won Wai-ching, Dr. Jeme Tien-yau, Chung Mun-yew, Tong Kai-son, Dr. Kin Ta-ting, Liang Pao-shi, Kwong Young-kong, Luk Hin-shen, Willy Tseng, Liu Yu-lin.

Captain Yung Leang as a teacher at the Foochow Naval School, 1883.

A reunion of the students in China, 1905. Front row: Tsai Shou-kee, Fong Pah-liang, Liu Chia-chew, Loo Yu-tang, Shen Ke-shu, and Liang Meng-ting. Second row: Sir Shouson Chow (Hong Kong), Yang Sew-nan, Admiral Tsai Ting-kan. Top row: Tsao Ka-hsiang, Yung Leang, Tong Shao-yi, Liang Tun-yen, Wong Liang-ting.

A reunion of the students in China, 1919.

Admiral Tsai Ting-kan.

A group of former students on the stairway of the Outlook Kiosk of the Customs Taotal Yamen, Tientsin. From top downward: Tong Shao-yi, Y. K. Kwong, Loo Yu-tong, Sir Shouson Chow, Tsai Shou-kee, Liang Tun-yen, Tsao Ka-hsiang, Yang Sew-an, Liu Yu-lin (ex-minister to London).

Woo Ying-fu at the age of 18.

Admiral Woo Ying-fu taken in Peking, 1914.

Yung Wing's wife, (Mary Kellogg) at the time of her marriage, 1876.

Yung Wing in 1907.

Woo Yang-tsang, age 14.   Woo Yang-tsang in his official dress.

Staff of the first Chinese embassy in the United States, Washington, D.C., 1900.

Tong King-sing, founder of the China Merchants Steam Navigation Co.

Chang Chih-tung, one of the great reformers of the 19th century.

Yuan Shih-k'ai, President of the Chinese Republic, 1912-1916.

Wu T'ing-fan, educated in England.

Liang Tun-yen.

Tong Shao-yi.

The Misses Mary and Margaret Bartlett on their visit to China, 1911.

鍾 周 溫 容 丁 鄺 唐 蘇 周 陶 吳
文 傳 蓋 尚 艦 炳 紹 鋭 長 協 偉
紫 正 東 輝 崇 元 少 劍 書 庭 仲
垣 卿 臣 珊 仙 亮 川 儀 侯 齡 臣 華 唐 賢 卿

The last reunion of the C.E.M. boys, 1936. Front row, left to right: Mr. Chung
Mun-yew, former director of Shanghai-Nanking Railway; Mr. B. C. Won, Super-
intendent of Soochow Customs; Mr. Ting Sung-kih; Mr. Tong Shao-yi, former
Premier; Sir Shouson Chow, First Premier of the Republic and delegate to the
Coronation of King Edward VIII in 1937; and Mr. Woo Chung-yen. Back row,
left to right: Mr. Chou Cheng-chin, Mr. Yung Shang-chien, Mr. Kwong Pin-kong,
Mr. Sue Sui-chao and Mr. Tao Ting-king. (The average age of the group was 76.)

Chang Chih-tung died in October 1909, after a career marked by the advocacy and introduction into China of educational, industrial, and military reforms. In fact, his famous "Exhortation to Learn" was long considered the bible of the reformers. Under his influence Wuch'ang and Hankow became great industrial centers supplying China with a great deal of her iron and steel. It is not without significance that the revolution of 1911 began in the industrialized Wu-Han area.

Although from time to time Chang Chih-tung revealed the true Confucian mandarin beneath his outward cloak of reformer, he seems never to have lost sight of the necessity that China should work in harmony with Occidental Powers and adopt Occidental industrial techniques. Somewhere in his entourage there was a guiding influence which kept him close to the path of reform. This might well have been Liang Tun-yen.

As was true of Tong Shao-yi, Liang's own career began to reveal itself more clearly after 1900. In 1904 he was appointed Chief of Customs at Hankow but, after a short period of service there, he was delegated to succeed Tong Shao-yi as Chief Magistrate at Tientsin. While in Tientsin he constantly strove to improve Peiyang University and to encourage many of its students to go to the United States to finish their education. In 1907 he was appointed Comptroller General of the Imperial Maritime Customs. Shortly after this appointment, he entered the Ministry of Foreign Affairs, first as Vice President of the Board and later as President.

As President of the Foreign Office, Liang Tun-yen negotiated the agreement with the American Minister, W. W. Rockhill, for the return of the Boxer Indemnity funds which had been paid to the United States Government. As a part of the plan to use the remitted indemnity to send students abroad, Liang Tun-yen established Tsing Hua College.

The college was situated on the outskirts of Peking in the former hunting park of Prince Tun. Established to give preparatory training to the students who were to be sent to the United States, it since has become one of the most famous educational institutions in Eastern Asia and from its gates have gone forth a constant stream of highly selected Chinese youths to the higher educational establishments of America. A glance through the *Who's Who for China* will reveal instantly the tremendous influence Tsing Hua has played in the creation of modern China. Its graduates fill important positions in every field of Chinese life.

The Boxer Indemnity plan for sending students to be educated in the United States follows closely the lines of the original Yung Wing Educational Mission and can be said to be a logical outgrowth of that earlier effort. The first president of Tsing Hua was Tong Kai-son. A member of the second detachment of the Educational Mission, he came to the United States in 1873. He spent one year at Yale before the Mission was recalled. For ten years he was Secretary of the K'aiping Mining Company at Tongshan. Later he entered the services of the Imperial Railways Administration. He died in 1913, shortly after the opening of Tsing Hua University. Again, we have in his case a direct connection between the little group of students who in 1840 made up the first class of the Morrison Educational Society School in Canton and the reform movement of the latter part of the nineteenth century, for Tong Kai-son was a son of Tong King-sing, one of the six students of the Morrison school.

As head of the Foreign Office, one of Liang Tun-yen's most difficult tasks was to represent the Chinese Government in the exceedingly troublesome and tangled Hukuang railway concession. This concession typified the impasse to which the concession hunting proclivities of the foreign powers had brought the Chinese Government. Emphasis upon legal rights, often doubtfully obtained but backed by diplomatic pressure, caused the foreign nations to block rather than to advance China's efforts at building railroads.

The Hukuang concession was a comparatively simple affair when it was first granted, but as time went on and each nation strove by diplomatic means to obtain a greater and greater share in the rights to finance and build the railways which were projected by the concession, it became so involved as literally to die of its own complexities. Originally, the concession had been granted to the American-China Development Company for the purpose of building a railway between Hankow and Canton. The Company was very slow to take advantage of its contract and by 1905 had completed only some thirty miles of line. Furthermore, the Company had engendered a great distrust among the local gentry of Canton by permitting a Belgian Syndicate, which had earlier attempted to get the concession, to obtain control of the Company through the purchase of a majority of the stock. As the Belgian Syndicate was only a very thin cover for French interests, it seemed that the American Company by a deliberate act of bad faith had permitted French political influence to be extended in Kuangtung and Kuangsi. This was the very contingency that the Cantonese had feared in the first place. To ward it off, they had deliberately given the concession to American interests rather than to the Belgians. In 1905 the provincial government of Canton, fearing the evil results of this undercover French influence, bought the property of the American Company and cancelled the concession for the sum of $6,750,000 gold. These funds were obtained by a loan from the government of the Hong Kong colony under the condition that if China subsequently needed foreign capital to finish the line, preference would be given to British interests. A mixed British and Chinese corporation now attempted to get the Canton provincial authorities to lend them the funds to complete the line. At this juncture Chang Chih-tung succeeded Yüan Shih-k'ai as the head of the Imperial Government in Peking and he, always pro-German in his sympathies, granted the concession to the Deutsche-Asiatische Bank. This was tantamount to permitting the Germans to penetrate into what the British presumed was their special sphere of interest in South China. The usual results followed. Protests on the part of the British and French Governments resulted in the Chinese Government's rearranging the concession so as to admit the financial interests of all three powers. The concession was now enlarged to include not only the Canton-Hankow line but a line from Hankow to Szechuan.

This prompted the American Government to bring forth a very vague promise which had been given to the American Minister in 1904 that in case the Chinese Government ever decided to build a railway line into Szechuan, British and American capital would be given an equal chance to bid for the concession. The American Government now began to push vigorously for an American share in the concession.

This was the situation that confronted Liang Tun-yen when he came to the presidency of the Foreign Office. There seems to be no doubt that the American Government was more solicitous to see that the loan should be made on terms that would not menace the administrative integrity and financial security of the Chinese Government than it was to secure a concession for American banking interests. Nevertheless, the record of the Americans in the original Canton-Hankow railway agreement was not such as to cause the Chinese to look with favor upon American interference. Liang Tun-yen realized the good intentions of the American Government, but at the same time he had to shoulder the blame for the inevitable delay that the American claim to share in the concession caused. It almost brought him to the breaking point with his chief, Chang Chih-tung, who became highly impatient and would have brushed aside the American claim in order to get the railways started. The death of Chang in October 1909 left Liang Tun-yen alone to handle this exceedingly involved and disagreeable situation.

As we might expect, Willard Straight was the Peking representative of the American banking interests. He regarded this concession, as he had the Manchurian loan, with a curious mingling of idealism for the future of China and practicality in seeking the huge profits which would accrue to the concessionaires.

Eventually, the difficulties narrowed down to two chief ones. The first was the American insistence upon receiving an equal share in the loan and an equal share in the construction and supply of materials for the lines. Secondly, Liang Tun-yen knew that the temper of the Chinese people was such that if the line were extended into either Hunan or Szechuan, popular outbreaks of a considerable proportions would ensue. He also knew that the Imperial Government was without the power to suppress such uprisings. He was caught in a predicament from which there seemed no escape. Even if he were to arrange a settlement which would be satisfactory to the British, French, German, and American interests, he knew that the construction of the line would be the signal for the long expected revolution to break out.

The various Governments concerned seemed not to have realized the danger inherent in the situation, and although Liang Tun-yen repeatedly warned them of the imminent danger of a widespread uprising, the contract for the loan was pushed through and signed in May, 1911. The immediate result was the outbreak of serious disorders in Szechuan, which in turn were followed by further disorders in Canton, Changsha, and Wuchang. The people, incensed at this bargaining away of Chinese rights, were convinced that the high officials in the capital, and particularly Shen Kung-pao, the Minister of Communications, were doing this at the sacrifice of their local provincial autonomy. Because the independence of the provinces, particularly in the matter of railway building, was the last safeguard of the Chinese people against the follies of the Manchu Court, they were determined to preserve this last bulwark.

The rebellion in Szechuan led directly into the revolution of 1911 and the downfall of the dynasty. Much of the anger of the provinces in the matter of the Hukuang loan was directed against America. This increased the difficulties of Liang Tun-yen, who was suspected by the Chinese of being pro-American. On the other hand, the American bankers thought that he was stubbornly holding up railway enterprise in China. His situation in this instance was typical of the experiences of China's first returned students. Beginning with Yung Wing, all of them found themselves attempting to build a bridge between two totally different worlds. The inevitable result was that they gained neither the gratitude of the Occidental world of machines and railways and progress nor that of the Chinese world of handicrafts and junks and conservatism. As to the Hukuang railways, not only did the bickerings of the Occidental nations over the concession directly aid in bringing on the revolution of 1911, but it also resulted in the actual building of the lines being postponed for many years. The railway between Canton and Hankow was not completed until September 1936, and then solely by Chinese efforts. To this day, no railway line has penetrated the great populous province of Szechuan.

In 1910 Liang Tun-yen was entrusted by the Imperial Court with a secret mission to Germany and the United States. This mission was, in effect, a second attempt to accomplish the aims of the secret mission of Tong Shao-yi in 1908. Liang's mission failed, as did that of Tong Shao-yi, but through no fault of the envoy. The Manchu house was now too far gone to be aided by any European alliances, and this state of affairs seems to have been more apparent to the Foreign Offices of Berlin and London than it was to Peking. The failure of both missions in no way eclipses the fact that, after thirty years of struggles against disheartening jealousy and opposition, it was the Yung Wing boys to whom the Court turned in its last bid for foreign support. Tong Shao-yi, the "Ajax" of Hartford days, and Liang

Tun-yen, the great south-paw pitcher of the "Orientals", had more than fulfilled the promise of that classroom in early Canton when Yung Wing, Tong King-sing, Woo Hsing, and Woo Fung stumbled through their first lessons in the learning of the "foreign devils".

Specifically, Liang Tun-yen's mission was to secure a loan from the United States for currency reform and industrial developments in Manchuria. In Berlin aid was to be secured in reorganizing the army and from both the United States and Germany there was to be secured a pledge to safeguard the territorial integrity of China. The accord concluded between Russia and Japan in 1910, which looked forward to the division of Manchuria between them, made the success of Liang's mission of vital significance to the integrity of the Chinese Empire. In the matter of the currency loan, Liang did secure the assent of Morgan and Company to undertake the loan. In turn this later led to American participation in the International Consortium loan of 1911, and a consequent modification of its terms in favor of China.

In Berlin, Liang was greatly encouraged by the sympathetic attitude of the German Government. He raised again the proposal of Tong Shao-yi that the German and American Governments should join in a declaration asserting their intention to preserve the territorial integrity of China. This meant that the two powers thereby would give notice to Russia and Japan to refrain from actually seizing Manchuria. In Washington in the spring of 1911, Liang Tun-yen found himself, as the Chinese so aptly phrase it, "whipping a featherbed". His mission became enmeshed in the tangle of international politics, most of the elements of which were kept from him. Neither the currency loan nor the plan for a declaration of territorial integrity seemed to make any headway. Finally it became clear that the American Government, although professing deep concern for the welfare of the Chinese Government and people, was really much more interested in preserving its good relations with the European powers and Japan than it was in preserving the territorial integrity of China. Great plans for the development of China were again sacrificed to the exigencies of international politics, politics in which China seemed always to receive the least consideration. In the meantime the Manchu dynasty was rapidly heading for the abyss. Before Liang could return to China, the Manchus had fallen before the storm of revolution. It is an ironic comment on Liang's mission that his last official act was to urge the American Government to stand for joint action on the part of the Occidental powers in preserving life and property in revolutionary China in order to ward off "the danger of selfish independent action on the part of any one of them."

Mention has already been made of the good fortune which attended the Chinese Educational Mission students who became associated with Yüan Shih-k'ai in Korea. After the Sino-Japanese war, Yüan returned to China to become governor of Shantung and in 1901, upon the death of Li Hung-chang, he succeeded Li as Viceroy of Chihli. It will be recalled that about this time Tong Shao-yi began his brilliant career. His first important appointment was that of Taotai or Chief Magistrate at Tientsin, a position which entailed the responsibility for supervising the relations between the Chinese and the foreigners in the Chihli viceroyalty.

When Tong left this post to go to Tibet as Special Commissioner for the Chinese Government, he was succeeded at Tientsin by another of the Yung Wing students. This was Liang Yu-ho (M. T. Liang) whose career has already been mentioned. Liang Yu-ho married one of Tong Shao-yi's daughters, and as Tong was the nephew of Tong King-sing, the old schoolmate of Yung Wing back in the early Canton days, we have illustrated here the tendency of the Chinese to strengthen their group interests by the ties of marriage. Liang Yu-ho had six children, four sons and two daughters. Two of his sons he sent to England to study medicine, and at present they are prominent physicians in Tientsin where they have one of the most modernly equipped private hospitals in China. His other two sons were educated in the United States, one being a physician and the other an accomplished artist.

Liang Yu-ho, in turn, was succeeded at Tientsin by Tsai-Shou-kee. Tsai, another Cantonese, was one of the first students Yung Wing chose to be sent to America. Arriving in America in 1872 as a member of the first detachment, he attended the Hartford Primary School and in 1875 entered the Hartford High School. He finished the prescribed four years course and from Hartford went to Yale University. Returning to China in 1881, he at first served as interpreter in the yamen of the Commissioner of Customs at Shanghai. Later he held a minor position in the office of the China Merchants Steam Navigation Company, and for a short time he was translator for the Great Northern Telegraph Company.

In 1886 good fortune took Tsai Shou-kee to Korea where he entered the service of Yüan Shih-k'ai as one of the latter's private secretaries. In 1903 Tsai returned to China to become the Director of the Peiyang Bureau of Foreign Affairs. This was the Foreign Affairs section of the Viceroyalty of Chihli and, in fact, was almost as important in the conduct of foreign affairs as was the Foreign Office of the Imperial Government in Peking. In 1904 Tsai Shou-kee became the president of Peiyang University at Tientsin, and in 1907 he succeeded Liang Yu-ho as Customs Commissioner at Tientsin, a post he retained until 1910. Just before being appointed to Tientsin, he followed Liang Yu-ho in another important post, the Customs Commissioner at the Manchurian port of Newchang. It will be recalled that Liang was appointed to this post, one heretofore always reserved for a Manchu, to negotiate with the Japanese for the retrocession of the Liaotung Peninsula, which they had

133

seized in the war with Russia. When Liang was transferred to Tientsin and then to Shanghai, Tsai was sent to Manchuria to preserve Chinese rights in South Manchuria. For his service there, he received the button of the first grade, an unusual distinction for a Chief of Customs.

In 1910 Tsai retired, and during the remainder of his life he devoted himself to charitable enterprises and to the improvement and expansion of Peiyang University. He died in Tientsin on May 23, 1933, survived by seven sons and seven daughters. His funeral was a magnificent affair in the best Buddhist traditions. It was also made noteworthy by the attendance of many prominent persons from the foreign community in North China. A detachment of the British Municipal Police marched in the procession; the flags in the British Concession were flown at half-mast and the coffin was followed by the Chairman and Councillors of the British Municipal Council. Tsai was the first Chinese ever to be elected to the Council on which he served in 1898, 1899, and 1900.

Another of Yüan's proteges was Chow Chang-ling, better known as Sir Shouson Chow of Hong Kong. He was fourteen years of age when he arrived in the United States in 1873. He attended the local grammar school at Winstead, Connecticut. Later he went to Phillips Academy at Andover, Massachusetts, and was graduated from there in 1881. He entered Columbia University but the recall of the Mission prevented him from pursuing his studies there beyond a few months.

Shortly after he returned to China, he accompanied Baron Von Mollendorf to Korea. Sir Shouson Chow remained in the Korean Customs until 1894, when he was transferred to the Chinese Consular service in Korea. In 1897 he returned to China to become the Managing Director of the China Merchants Steam Navigation Company, which it will be recalled, was formed in 1874 by Li Hung-chang at the suggestion of Yung Wing and Tong King-sing. Yung Wing saw that if the

Chinese did not attempt to meet the foreigners on their own grounds, the commerce of China's great inland rivers would fall entirely into the hands of foreign interests. It was the hope of the directors of the Company that the Imperial Government could be induced to give it a monopoly of trade at the ports which were not yet opened by treaty and also to give it a monopoly of the transport of grain to the capital. However, the fear of the Court of giving offence to the foreigners prevented the Company from being granted these favors. Nevertheless, the China Merchants grew until it possessed a large fleet of steam vessels and was able to draw a great deal of the coastal trade into its hands.

With the exception of one or two ports opened by treaty, the inland river traffic remained in the hands of the Chinese until 1898. In that year many of the river ports were opened to the traffic of foreign vessels. The first steam launch to ascend the Yangtze as far as Chunking did so in 1898, and by 1900 a regular steam service was inaugurated through the Yangtze gorges to Ichang. Both these enterprises were undertaken by foreigners. In fact, the very danger that Yung Wing anticipated in 1868 when he first suggested the formation of a Chinese steamship company, rapidly came about after the foreigners had once forced their way into the vast inland rivers of China. This commerce, together with the coastal commerce, rapidly fell under the control of a few great foreign firms, with only the China Merchants Steam Navigation Company standing between them and a complete monopoly.

It was to the China Merchants Company that Sir Shouson Chow brought his flare for business. Between 1897 and 1903, under his able management, the Company prospered and expanded until it possessed the largest fleet of merchant vessels in the Far East. In 1903 he left the China Merchants to become Managing Director of the Peking-Mukden Railway, succeeding Liang Yu-ho (M. T. Liang), in this important position. In

1907 Sir Shouson Chow followed Tsai Shou-kee as Customs Commissioner at Newchang in Manchuria. Tsai, in turn, had succeeded Liang Yu-ho at Newchang. Newchang was the most critical place in Manchuria as it was here that the Japanese and Chinese interests were most likely to clash. All three of these were chosen because of their ability to handle such a crucial situation, and their appointment to Newchang illustrates how the Manchu government was coming to depend upon these American educated officials as "trouble shooters" at the most critical points of contact with the other nations.

In 1910 Sir Shouson Chow was appointed Councillor in the Foreign Office in Peking. On the outbreak of the revolution of 1911, he retired to Hong Kong, where he commenced a long and distinguished career as representative of the Chinese community in the British colony. In 1917 he was made Justice of the Peace in Hong Kong, and in 1921 a member of the Legislative Council of the colony. In 1926 he was appointed Chinese representative on the Hong Kong Executive Council, the first Chinese to be so honored. In the same year he was knighted by the Crown for his distinguished services to the colony of Hong Kong. He is still active in business affairs, but he devotes most of his energies to various projects designed to better the condition of the numerous Chinese population of Hong Kong.

Woo Chung-yen, known among his schoolmates in the Hartford days as "Big Nose," also was sent to Korea with Von Mollendorf. In 1883, when China established a regular Consular service in Korea, he became Vice Consul at Jenchuan and later Consul at Yuensan. At the end of the Sino-Japanese War, Woo returned to China to assist Yüan Shih-k'ai in the formation of the modern army that was being organized. After the Boxer troubles of 1900, he was sent to Germany with the special mission of Prince Chun. This mission was sent upon the demand of the Kaiser who wanted the Chinese to apologize publicly for the murder of Baron Von Kettler during the Boxer uprising.

136

When Woo returned to China, he was assigned to the Consular service. He served as Consul in Kobe and Osaka and later he became Consul General in Yokohama, the most important Consular post in the Chinese service. After six years in this post, he was sent to Mexico to negotiate an indemnity from the Mexican Government for the death of over one hundred Chinese killed during the Mexican Revolution of 1911. Woo was successful and was able to get President Madero to agree to pay China an indemnity of over $3,000,000. The amount was small, but it was noteworthy in that it marked a departure from the usual procedure whereby China found herself on the paying rather than the receiving end of such indemnity claims.

During the World War, Woo was appointed director of the Bureau for the Repatriation of Enemies and the Sequestration of Enemy Property. The expulsion of the Germans and Austrians from China was a task the Chinese did not like as they realized that the attempt to get China into the war on the side of the Allies was intended chiefly to eliminate German trade competition in China. Most of the German citizens in China were engaged in philanthropic and missionary enterprises rather than in business, but no distinction was made in the deportation proceedings between these and the German business men. As a consequence, the Chinese were reluctant to expel the Germans in such a wholesale manner. Woo's conduct of the Repatriation Bureau reflected this Chinese opinion, and it was noted rather for the mild way in which he handled the Germans rather than for any desire to expel them. In fact, the Germans were not expelled from China until after the Armistice of November, 1918, and then only under extreme pressure from the Allied Governments. Within a year of the signing of the peace treaty, the Chinese permitted the Germans to return to China as they had no desire to eliminate the check which German business men gave to the British and French. Woo Chung-yen's last post was that of Director of the Bureau of

Emigration, which he held from 1924 to 1928, when he retired. He still lives in retirement in Shanghai.

Sir Shouson Chow was not the first Chinese to be honored with a British title, for many years before another of the members of the Educational Mission had received the K.C.M.G. from the British Crown. This was Sir Chun Tung Liang Shing or Liang Pe-yuk, to give his name in the Cantonese dialect. He acquired his title in 1897 at the time of Queen Victoria's Jubilee in commemoration of the sixtieth year of her reign. Liang was appointed First Secretary to Prince Chun, who was designated to represent the Chinese Government at the Jubilee. The Jubilee was considered an appropriate time for the somewhat wholesale distribution of honors and Liang was included among those who received titles. He seems to have been the first Chinese ever to have received an order of knighthood from the British Crown. Later, Liang was Chinese Minister to Berlin, and, from 1903 to 1907, he served as Chinese Minister in Washington.

Several other members of the Educational Mission found careers in the Chinese Consular and Diplomatic service. When the students first returned to China, the Chinese foreign service was only a few years old and China still had no representatives at the capitals of the smaller countries. The emigration of Chinese to the various parts of the world brought on the necessity for diplomatic and consular representation and with the development of these services, the knowledge of the Occident possessed by the Educational Mission students made them logical appointees for posts in foreign countries. Only a few, however, reached the highest posts of Minister or Ambassador as such positions were usually given to Chinese prominent in domestic politics rather than career members of the consular and diplomatic services.

The first attempts of China to send representatives abroad began in 1866, with the despatch to Europe of Ping Chun. Ping was a Manchu official, who held a position of only minor importance, and his mission was nothing more than that of going to "take a look-see" in order to inform the Court of conditions in Europe. He seems to have viewed with great disfavor Europe with its machinery and cities and noise. He also entertained a very low opinion of the morality of European society. In consequence, his report was not such as to encourage the Chinese Government to send any further envoys abroad. The next attempt to have China represented abroad came in 1868, with the mission of Anson Burlingame to the United States and to Europe. Burlingame had served as the American Minister at Peking from 1861 to 1867. When in 1867 he resigned his post as American Minister, he was asked by some of the leading officials in the Chinese Government to represent China in a mission to the foreign governments. Burlingame accepted with obvious pleasure as during his stay in Peking he had become enthusiastic about the future of China and believed that the time was ripe for China to enter into a series of mutually beneficial treaties with the various nations. These were to take the place of the one-sided treaties forced upon China as a consequence of her defeats in the wars of 1842 and 1856. His mission resulted in the Burlingame treaty of 1868 between the United States and China and its equalitarian character led directly to the establishment of Yung Wing's Chinese Educational Mission to the United States.

Mr. Burlingame was not so fortunate in concluding treaties with the European countries as he had been with the United States and his death in St. Petersburg in 1868 brought his mission to an end.

The Burlingame mission did reveal to the Chinese the necessity of establishing permanent diplomatic representatives abroad, and in 1875 a start was made by appointing Kuo Sungtao Chinese Minister to London. Shortly after this, legations were established in Washington, Paris, Berlin, and St. Petersburg. Chen Lan-pin and Yung Wing, the Commissioners in charge of the Educational Mission, were accredited to Washington as China's first Ministers to the United States. With the establishment of legations, consular offices were opened wherever there were enough Chinese to justify them.

When the abandonment of the Chinese Educational Mission was being considered, the last Commissioner, Woo Tzê-têng, suggested that several students be attached to the various legations as interpreters and secretaries. Although his idea was not carried out in any systematic way, some of the students did find their way into the legations at Washington, London, and Paris. Yung Kwai, a nephew of Yung Wing, was such a one. It will be recalled that he was one of the boys who became a Christian and who refused to return to China when the Mission was recalled. Apparently the Chinese Government soon forgave him for his disobedience because in 1884 he was appointed secretary in the Chinese Legation at Washington. He served in the Washington Legation for the next fifty years. He retired in 1933 and now lives with his wife and family in Washington, D. C.

Liu Yu-lin was another of the students who was assigned to the diplomatic service. He returned to China in 1881 and at first was placed in the Telegraph School in Tientsin, but in 1882 he was sent to the Chinese Consulate in New York. From there he was transferred in 1884 to the Chinese Legation in Washington. Afterwards he served successively as Consul General in the Straits Settlement, Secretary of the Legation in London, Charge d'Affaires at Brussels, Consul General in South Africa, Vice Minister of Foreign Affairs, and from 1910 to 1914 as Minister to Great Britain.

Chang Hon-yen was one of the few students who returned to the United States upon his own initiative expressly to complete his education. When the Mission was recalled, he had finished the first year of a law course at Yale College. He did not remain in China but almost immediately returned to the

140

United States and finished his legal studies in 1883. He practiced law in San Francisco, and undoubtedly was the first Chinese to practice law in the United States. For some years he served as Consul General in Vancouver and later as Consul General in San Francisco.

Ouyang King was another member of the Mission who spent his entire career in the foreign service of the Chinese Government. He came to the United States in 1872 with the first contingent and when the Mission was recalled, he had already been graduated from the Sheffield Scientific School at Yale College. Upon his return to China he was sent to the Foochow Naval School, but in 1883 he returned to the United States and entered the Chinese Consulate in New York. In 1884 he became Consul in San Francisco, and from 1907 to 1910 he was Consul General at Panama. From 1912 to 1921 he served as Consul General at Batavia, and, after a short interim as Charge in the London Legation, he represented China as Minister to Chile until 1928. He died in Peking early in 1941.

Despite the fact that during their ten years in the United States the majority of the Educational Mission students became very much Americanized, only a few of them forgot their obligations to the Chinese Government to the extent of renouncing China and remaining in thé United States. Yet the attractions of American life must have been very great for most of the boys, particularly after their chagrin at the indifferent reception accorded them when they returned to China. Of those who did remain or, shortly after their recall to China, returned to the United States, only three seem to have completely divorced themselves from any service to the Chinese Government.

One of these, Lee Kwai-pan, engaged in the tea business in New York, but he died a few years after the abandonment of the Mission. The other two carved out modest careers in the

141

American environment. One of them, Jang Ting-seong, seems to have been determined to return to the United States, for when in 1883 Tong Shao-yi boarded the official junk which was to take him to Korea to join Von Mollendorf in the Korean Customs service, he found Jang hiding as a stowaway aboard the junk. Jang had no knowledge that this was the junk designated to take Tong to Korea but had boarded it under the belief that it was bound for Java and Sumatra. From one of these places he hoped to get to the United States. When he recognized his former schoolmate now arrayed in his mandarin robes, Jang emerged from his hiding place and made himself known to Tong. Tong took him to Korea and from there enabled him to get passage to America. Jang subsequently became well known in New York as a consulting engineer, and was one of the engineers who designed and erected the Brooklyn Bridge. He invented the Jann coupling for railway cars and many other mechanical devices. He was at one time Manager of the Dry Storage Battery Company of Brooklyn, New York, and also consulting Engineer of the Croton Water Works of New York. He died some years ago in New York City.

Lee Yen-fu, better known in America as Yen Fu-lee, was another of the students who made a permanent home in the United States. He was the author of the widely read children's book, "When I was a Boy in China". He made his living as a journalist and for several years was the editor of a newspaper in New Jersey. In 1917 he attained some notice by writing a new version of the "Star Spangled Banner." For some years he was managing editor of the *American Banker*. In 1933 he returned to China to become editor of the *Canton Gazette*, a bilingual newspaper. He was married twice, in 1887 to Elizabeth Maud Jerome, and in 1897 to Sophie F. Bolles. During the World War one of his sons, Gilbert Jerome, was killed in action at Berdinal, France.

One of the most surprising facts about Yung Wing's "Americans" is the almost total absence among them of the revolutionary tendencies which became so prominent in China after 1900. Despite the decided lack of enthusiasm shown towards them on the part of the Mandarinate when they first returned to China, they seemed never to have lost a deep sense of loyalty and obligation towards the Manchu dynasty. Only when the coming of the republic could no longer be forestalled did any of them show any signs of changing their allegiance, and this seems to have been motivated more by the higher patriotism they felt towards China than by any spirit of opportunism. Their absence from the ranks of revolutionary groups is almost complete. In only one instance do we find one of the former Educational Mission students actively connected with any revolutionary party prior to the actual establishment of the republic in 1912. This was Yung Sing-kew, better known by his Cantonese name of Hoy Yung. He was one of the students assigned to the Naval School at Tientsin, but he soon resigned to go into business. In 1891, while in Hong Kong, he met Sun Yat-sen, then a medical student at the Alice Memorial Hospital there. Sun persuaded Hoy to become a member of the Tung Ming Hui, the revolutionary party formed by Sun Yat-sen and other revolutionists. Thereafter he seems to have contributed liberally from his private fortune to the party, for he had become quite wealthy in the tea business in Hankow.

In 1899 he took part in a plot to remove Chang Chih-tung, the Viceroy of Hunan and Hupei provinces. The plot proved abortive and Hoy had to flee for his life. He now entered actively in the revolutionary cause and established the *China Daily News* to promote revolutionary sentiment in South China. When in 1911 the revolution was crowned with success, Hoy hastened to Nanking to take part in the new government. He was soon disillusioned, however, by the welter of party politics which swirled around him. He thenceforth renounced all participation in the new republic and returned to Hong Kong where he spent the next ten years engaged in many business enterprises, the most important of which was the organization of the Chinese-Siam Steamship Company. He died on May 7, 1933.

There are many others of the Chinese Educational Mission whose careers were cast on a smaller scale than those who have been mentioned in these pages. In many instances they died young before they could attain any distinction. In a few instances they disappeared shortly after their return to China and left behind them no clue as to their whereabouts or the experiences which life in China brought to them. For the most part, however, China's first hundred amply repaid the radical departure from the accustomed mores which occurred when the Imperial Government took the unprecedented step of sending a band of Chinese youths to America to learn something of the knowledge of the "barbarian" West.

CHAPTER IX

REVOLUTION AND REPUBLIC

One would suppose that the revolution of 1911 which ushered in the Chinese Republic would have resulted in a very favorable turn in the fortunes of Yung Wing's "Americans". For thirty years this small band of pioneers of westernization had been at the very center of every attempt to introduce into China the technical achievements of the Occidental world. In every telegraph, railway, or mining enterprise upon which the Chinese government embarked we find them slowly but surely working their way up the long ladder of official preferment until finally in all such enterprises they either stood at the top or supplied the technical skill and energy which made these ventures possible.

In politics, also, they showed a skill and ability which enabled them to meet the old type mandarins on their own ground and more and more to wrest from them the most important offices in the Imperial Government. In fact, J. O. P. Bland, a contemporary of the events described in this book and a most caustic critic of modern China, says that by 1911 the "Cantonese clique" of Tong Shao-yi, Liang Tun-yen, Liang Yu-ho, Wu T'ing-fan, and other western-educated officials exercised such great influence that they were the ones who really brought the republic into being. He believes that without the active aid of this group, all of whom were saturated with republicanism despite their long service to the Manchus, it would have been impossible for Sun-Yat-sen and the other revolutionary leaders to establish the republic.

It is true that the advent of the republic did temporarily add further luster to the careers of some of the more prominent of the former students of the Educational Mission, but, in general, it spelled misfortune for most of them and an early disappearance from official life. Under the republic they were caught between two irreconcilable forces in much the same way they had been caught during the empire. Under the Imperial Government they had to stand between the foreigners and the mandarinate of old China. Now they soon found themselves caught between the radicalism of the republican leaders and the monarchical ambitions of Yüan Shih-k'ai. With neither could they find themselves in agreement. The result was that after a short spell of brilliance in the new political sky, they disappeared from public life.

Tong Shao-yi played a most important role in bringing about the republican regime, but even he could not straddle the impassable gulf that separated the republican party from Yüan Shih-k'ai and his ambition to found a new dynasty.

When the revolution broke out, Liang Tun-yen was in Germany and Tong Shao-yi was in retirement in Tientsin. For several years Yüan Shih-k'ai had been acting the part of the "simple farmer" on his farm in Hunan, but like an old war horse, he was merely waiting for the first sound of strife to spring back into the political battle. The call for action came with the first revolutionary outbreak at Wuchang in October, 1911.

At first little notice was taken of the serious defection of Imperial troops in the great industrial Wu-Han area, but when, within the month of October, the Yangtze cities of Wuchang, Hanyang, and Hankow fell into the hands of the rebels, it began to look as if the long expected revolution had at last come about. The first sign of real concern on the part of the Manchu court was shown when Yüan was recalled from retirement and appointed Viceroy of the two provinces of Hupei and Hunan. It was hoped that by this move he would be able to keep loyal some of the most modern troops which, before his retirement, Yüan had organized and armed with modern weapons. Moreover, the diplomatic corps in Peking, in conjunction with repre-

146

sentatives of the foreign banking groups who were just about to bring to a conclusion the negotiations for a large loan to the Manchu government, were looking for a strong man who could handle the situation and Yüan seemed to be the only one available.

Yüan now simulated a reluctance to leave his few acres of land in Hunan in order to save the empire. It soon became clear that he would not emerge until he was granted full authority to treat with the rebels. This was given him at the end of October, when he was appointed Imperial Commissioner with unlimited authority to restore order.

The true sympathies of Yüan Shih-k'ai at this critical juncture have been the cause of much speculation. Did he sincerely strive to save the Imperial rule or did he secretly work for the abdication of the Manchus? In fact, the choice was not as clear cut as this. He seems rather to have been the victim of circumstances over which he had very little control. When he arrived in Peking he found himself cut off from the currents of Chinese life and a prisoner of the isolation which had always characterized the Imperial Government in Peking. Immured in their vast palaces, the Manchu rulers were in no position to judge what was going on. They were completely dependent upon the reports of their subordinates out in the provinces. Yüan Shih-k'ai now found himself in this same isolated position. He knew very little of that which was taking place in the real centers of events in the Yangtze Valley and the Canton areas in South China. Despite his long career as a reformer, he was without any real understanding of the extent of the influences which had been steadily flowing into China from the West. In this dilemma, he was forced to place his reliance upon those who really understood these forces. Tong Shao-yi, who was his personal representative at Wuchang and Shanghai, became his sole contact with the revolutionists and Tong Shao-yi now gave full reign to the republican sympathies which he must have always felt, but which during thirty years of loyal service to the Manchus he had managed to suppress.

On December 8, 1911, Yüan despatched Tong to Hankow to treat with the revolutionists. In the meantime, a constitution had been hastily drawn up which reduced the emperor to a mere figurehead and actually gave complete power to Yüan Shih-k'ai. In the organization of China's first constitutional government it was noteworthy that most of the old line Chinese officials were passed over in favor of Tong Shao-yi, Liang Tun-yen, and others of the Educational Mission. In the new cabinet, Liang Tun-yen became Minister of Foreign Affairs, with Hu Wei-teh, another of the old Mission "boys", as Vice President of the Ministry. Tong Shao-yi was given the most important post of Minister of Communications, and he had Liang Yu-ho (M. T. Liang), whose career in the Imperial Railway Administration we have already mentioned, as Vice Minister. Admiral Sah Chen-ping, trained in the British Navy, was in charge of the Navy Board. Admiral Tsai Ting-kan, another of Yung Wing's "Americans", was dispatched to Wuchang to arrange an armistice with the revolutionists. In the composition of the new government, the Mission "boys" certainly came into their own. But their glory was to be short lived, as subsequent events will show.

Early in December, Tong Shao-yi was delegated by Yüan to proceed to Wuchang to open negotiations with the leaders of the revolution. He was accompanied by Captain Yung Leang, another former Educational Mission student. When Tong arrived at Hankow, his first act was to consent to have the seat of negotiations moved to Shanghai. In Shanghai, the revolutionists were represented by Wu T'ing-fan. Wu was a most interesting figure. He had been sent to England to be educated about the same time that Tong Shao-yi was being educated in the grammar and high schools of Hartford, Connecticut. Wu was a "made-in-England" counterpart of the "Americanized" Tong Shao-yi. He had served as Chinese Minister at Washington from 1896 to 1903 and again from 1908 to 1909. Into the hands of these two thoroughly "westernized" Chinese suddenly was thrust the fate of the Chinese empire, and from their hands there emerged the Chinese Republic.

How did this come about and what part did Tong Shao-yi play in this fateful decision? In the first place, when Tong arrived in Shanghai, he seems to have come to the conviction that the Manchu rule had run its course and that the only hope for China was a complete change of regime. Wu T'ing-fan had definitely cast in his lot with the revolutionists and was steadfast in his demand for the abdication of the Manchus and the setting up of a republic. In Tong, he seems to have found an opponent who already was converted to his point of view. From Shanghai, Tong began to send to Yüan Shih-k'ai, isolated in Peking, a stream of telegrams in which he stressed the utter hopelessness of resisting the demands for the abdication of the Emperor. He informed Yüan that his "private investigations show that popular feeling in the eastern and southern provinces is firmly established in favor of a republic and there is nothing to withstand the advance of this feeling." He advised the immediate promulgation of an Imperial decree convoking a National Assembly to decide the form of government and to arrange for a just and generous treatment of the Imperial family. Yüan, influenced by Tong's barrage of telegrams, issued a decree in which he said, "Let us adopt the suggestion made by Tong Shao-yi and submit the matter of the form of government to the vote of a National Assembly." Previous to the issuance of this decree, Tong, at Shanghai, already had agreed to four points which practically assured the victory of the revolutionists. He agreed to an extension of the armistice; to a withdrawal of Imperial troops from certain key areas, which was tantamount to an abandonment of Hankow and Hanyang to the revolutionists; to the convocation of a National Assembly to decide the form of government; and finally, he promised that, pending the decision of the Assembly, the Imperial Government would refrain from making any foreign loans. The last point was fatal to the Imperial cause as Yüan was without funds to pay his troops or to carry on the Imperial administration. Tong's action in agreeing to the above conditions was promptly repudiated by Yüan Shih-k'ai but it was too late to save the dynasty. By this time, Sun Yat-sen had arrived at Shanghai from Japan and he was determined to push through the abdication of the emperor. Sun's task was made much easier by the sympathy for the republican cause which Tong had exhibited. On February 12, 1912, Yüan, either no longer able to resist the forces around him, or not desiring to resist them, persuaded the Imperial Manchu family to make way for the Chinese Republic. Shortly thereafter, Yüan was elected President of the Republic and there was ushered in a long and unhappy struggle between him and the republican leaders for the control of the new government.

In his greed for power, Yüan soon drove Sun Yat-sen and his followers into exile. As for Yung Wing's "Americans," unacceptable to the republicans because of their long service to the Manchus and totally out of sympathy with Yüan Shih-k'ai's dynastic ambitions, they soon withdrew from public life to enjoy a well-earned retirement. Tong Shao-yi played a decisive part in bringing about the establishment of the republic. He also was responsible for the generous settlement which the republic made with the Manchu Imperial family. Early in the peace conference at Shanghai, he openly avowed his sympathy for the republican cause, but, at the same time, he insisted that just and honorable provisions should be made for the support of the Imperial family. In doing this, Tong not only wanted to provide for his former sovereign but he also wanted to show the Occidental nations that the Chinese, even in the midst of revolution, still could remember Mencius' tolerant doctrine of the "middle way." Perhaps Tong wanted to administer a rebuke to the western nations who at this moment were pressing China from all sides, particularly in the matter of currency and railway loans.

150

On February 15, 1912, Yüan Shih-k'ai was elected the first president of the Chinese Republic. Sun Yat-sen, who had been elected provisional president by the revolutionary government at Nanking, resigned in order to make way for Yüan, "the strong man" who everyone seemed to think could pull China out of the morass of difficulties in which she found herself. Tong was now definitely over on the side of the republic, and one of the first tasks entrusted to him was to head a delegation to Peking to invite Yüan to make a journey south to Nanking and Shanghai. The delegation also pressed the claims of the South that Nanking should be made the capital of the new republic, but just at this moment Yüan's troops in Peking got out of hand and engaged in an orgy of looting and killing. In the midst of these disturbances, the claims of the Nanking delegation were pushed aside with the result that Peking remained the capital.

By early March, order was restored and Yüan was able to get together the new republican government. In the cabinet, Tong Shao-yi became Premier, but the nomination of Liang Yu-ho (M. T. Liang) to be Minister of Communications was not accepted by the National Assembly. Neither would the Assembly accept Liang Tun-yen as Minister for Foreign Affairs. Both these vetoes on the part of the Assembly were significant as they clearly indicated that the Republican party of Sun Yat-sen, which dominated the Assembly, was going to have little use for Yung Wing's "Americans" despite their long years of service in the cause of the reform. Theirs was the fate of most pioneers. Once the trail has been broken, those who follow have little use for the trail-makers.

Tong Shao-yi also might have been rejected, but the National Assembly accepted him in the hope that he would be able to secure a foreign loan. As the new government was in dire need of funds, Tong recommended negotiations with the Banking Consortium representing the financial interests of

Great Britain, France, Germany, Russia, the United States, and Japan. In the midst of these negotiations, which promised to be protracted despite the desperate financial needs of the government, Tong turned to a Belgian Syndicate and borrowed from them the sum of $5,000,000. He also contracted with this same syndicate for further loans of several more million dollars. Of course, this raised an outcry on the part of the bankers and diplomats of the nations forming the Consortium. Tong was accused of bad faith, and such was the pressure brought by the diplomatic corps that further borrowings from the Belgian syndicate was made impossible. Tong's only course now was to attempt to work out with the Consortium a loan based on terms which would not impair the ability of the new republic to control its own finances. He did not want to see the republic stifled at its very birth in the meshes of foreign finance. Finding himself unable to accept the conditions upon which the bankers insisted that the loan should be made, in July, 1912, he resigned and retired to his home in Tientsin.

The later history of the loan negotiations with the Consortium is well known. Yüan Shih-k'ai, impatient at the unwillingness of the National Assembly to accept a loan on conditions which President Wilson described as gravely menacing the sovereignty of China, dissolved the Republican party and concluded the loan without the consent of the National Assembly. Despite the fact that such proceedings were clearly unconstitutional, Yüan was materially assisted in this course by the anxiety of the Consortium bankers to reap the huge profits which accrued to them from the Consortium loan. They also wanted a free hand in setting up such conditions that the security of their investment would be "legally" unquestionable. The new Republic, instead of starting off free from foreign control, found itself at the very outset entangled in the very same meshes of foreign finance which had so materially helped in the downfall of the old regime. It is no wonder that a few years later Paul Reinsch, the American Minister to China under the Wilson regime, found both Tong Shao-yi and Liang Tun-yen "displaying a gentle skepticism for all reforms."

After his resignation as Premier, Tong worked fitfully with the provisional government formed by Sun Yat-sen at Canton, but he soon faded from public life, and although pressed many times to resume public office, he remained steadfast in his refusal to take up again the burden of what must have seemed to him a well-nigh hopeless cause.

In the meantime Yüan Shih-k'ai was plotting to betray the republic for which he had never shown the slightest sympathy. By 1914 he had driven every element of opposition from public life and ruled as absolute dictator in Peking. Sun-Yat-sen and his followers, temporarily helpless to oppose Yüan, withdrew to Canton where a provisional government was established pending the time that Yüan could be overthrown.

At this juncture the World War broke out, an event which involved China in further difficulties. The presence of the fortified base of Germany at Kiaochow on the Shangtung coast made it difficult for China to keep the war from being carried to her soil. The Japanese used the presence of this base as the reason for entering the war. In the latter part of August, 1914, they threw a cordon of battleships around the German leasehold and then prepared to overcome the heavily fortified base by a land attack. Japanese troops were landed on the northern coast of Shantung and marched overland to attack the German forts from the rear. This action on the part of Japan violated Chinese neutrality, but the Japanese were determined to use the war as an excuse to get rid of the German leasehold on the Shantung coast. The government of Yüan Shih-k'ai protested but could do nothing to resist the Japanese occupation of Shantung. Early in November the German base of Kiaochow was surrendered to the Japanese, and thereafter Japan held this base and much of the hinterland of Shantung until the conclusion of the war.

The Japanese Government also decided to use the preoccupation of the European powers with the war to reduce China to a protectorate of Japan. Yüan was determined to carry through his monarchical plans and there is grave suspicion that he was willing to permit the Japanese to secure a dominating voice in China in return for their support of his plot to seat himself upon the Dragon throne. The Japanese move came early in 1915. The Chinese Government was suddenly presented with the notorious Twenty-one Demands, accompanied by a strong intimation that if the demands were not promptly accepted, military occupation of China would ensue. The demands were such that if they had been accepted the Chinese would have lost control of their economic resources, of their railways, of their military and naval forces, and of their independent diplomatic relations with other nations. Moreover, South Manchuria would have become, in everything but name, a Japanese colony.

There now ensued an upsurge of the fundamental spirit of independence which the Chinese people possess in a high degree, but which the misrule of the Manchus in modern times had obscured. By a nation-wide campaign of publicity, the Chinese people were fully informed of the menace to their independence. The result was that public opinion was aroused to a high degree of indignation and it became apparent that if the Japanese insisted upon forcing their demands upon China, the whole country would rise in resistance to them. In turn, the storm of public protest gave the Chinese negotiators the support they needed to stave off the Japanese demands. By using every opportunity for procrastination and by taking advantage of every loophole of Occidental legalism, the Chinese negotiators were able to whittle down the Japanese demands to such a point that little remained but the hollow shell of what the Japanese had originally demanded. The substance was literally negotiated away by the Chinese, and particularly by the brilliant diplomacy of the American-trained Wellington Koo.

During the protracted negotiations, the Chinese people gave ample evidence that from now on any one who attempted to bargain away their national heritage would have to reckon with the anger of the whole Chinese people. Despite this evident fact, Yüan Shih-k'ai, blind to everything except his own ambitions and totally unable or unwilling to realize the changing temper of the Chinese people, pushed through his plans for the reestablishment of the monarchy. He was encouraged in this by the support of France and Russia, both governments indicating that they would recognize the new regime if Yüan would bring China into the war on the side of the Allies. Curiously enough, it was Japan who stepped in at this moment and vetoed the change from a republic to a monarchy. Japan wanted China to enter the World War solely under her leadership and she was not yet ready to encourage China to take that step.

Even if Japan had consented to the pushing through of Yüan's monarchical designs, it is doubtful if they would have been crowned with success. When it became apparent that he was planning to betray the republic, revolt broke out in Szechuan and was rapidly followed by uprisings in most of the southern provinces. Despite this opposition, Yüan actually had himself proclaimed emperor, but his triumph was shortlived, for by early 1916 it became evident that the nation would not stand for this barefaced betrayal. Yüan was forced to renounce his ambitions, and in June, 1916, he died, largely as a result of the worry and humiliation he had suffered by the failure of his plans.

Liang Tun-yen, it will be recalled, was in Europe at the time of the 1911 revolution. He remained there until 1914, when Yüan Shih-k'ai persuaded him to return to take the post of Minister of Communications. Upon his return to China, Liang soon discovered Yüan's desire to make himself emperor. Not wishing to be involved in this scheme, he resigned all of his public offices and went into retirement. He did not appear

155

on the scene again until July, 1917, when, much to the amazement of everyone, both he and K'ang Yu-wei, the great reformer of 1898, emerged as participants in General Chang Hsün's attempt to restore to the throne the young Manchu Emperor, Hsüan T'ang.

Chang Hsün was a reactionary general of the old school who, in a rather naive way, thought that by restoring the Manchus to the throne he could settle the difficulties in which the republican government of China found itself. In the summer of 1917, he had been summoned to Peking to mediate between the various political cliques which were striving for control of the Central Government. Much to the embarrassment of everyone, he decided that the best solution of the problem would be to sweep aside all political groups and, by a coup d'etat, restore the Manchu dynasty to power. At this time, the young Manchu emperor was still enjoying his titles and personal perquisites as provided for in the Abdication Agreement of 1912. He was living in the Forbidden City in Peking. Suddenly at four o'clock in the morning of July 1, 1917, Chang Hsün appeared in the Imperial palace and seated the young lad upon the throne. He then proclaimed the new government, in which Liang Tun-yen was named Minister of Foreign Affairs.

What Liang's motives were in getting mixed up in this impracticable plot to restore the Manchu dynasty to the throne of China is not difficult to guess. When he returned to China in 1914, he found the revolution betrayed and Yüan Shih-k'ai ruling with an iron hand that brooked no opposition. Realizing the true state of affairs, he withdrew to retirement. Upon Yüan's death, the dictatorial power which he had exercised became divided among a group of militarists and politicians who, for unrestrained selfishness and willingness to sacrifice every national interest to the furtherance of their own ambitions, far exceeded anything the Manchus had done, even at the weakest period of their rule. Liang must have come to the conclusion

156

that China was not yet ready for a republic and that its salvation lay in the restoration of the Manchus. After all, he had served the Imperial family loyally for over thirty years and they had rewarded him with the highest honors at their bestowal. These then must have been the reasons which caused him to throw in his lot with the attempt of Chang Hsün to restore the emperor to the throne.

The coup d'etat no sooner took place than it became evident that it was doomed to failure. Chang Hsün evidently thought that the militarist clique which had been attempting to control the Peking Government would readily submit to the new order and would accept the titles and high positions which he was ready to offer them. In this he was mistaken. Common danger caused the militarists and politicians to forget their differences and to unite in a move to crush the restoration. Their combined forces attacked Peking and soon caused Chang Hsün to flee to the shelter of the Legation Quarter. A curious feature of the bombardment of Peking was the use for the first time in China of a military aeroplane. It dropped several bombs on the Forbidden City and also upon the Fêngtai railway station.

When it became apparent that the restoration would fail, Liang Tun-yen took refuge in the Dutch Legation and remained there for many months. When his life was no longer in danger, he left the Legation to retire to Tientsin. Only once again does his name flash across the pages of modern Chinese history and that in the most curious circumstances for one of the pioneer "westernizers" of China. Johnstone, the English tutor of the young emperor, Hsüan T'ang, tells in his very informative book *Twilight in the Forbidden City* of a reception held in the Forbidden City on December 5, 1922, in honor of the marriage of the young emperor to a Manchu princess. Members of the diplomatic corps in Peking, together with high officials of the Chinese Republic, were invited to attend the reception. The emperor and his bride were attended by two princesses, two ministers of the Court, and four other Chinese gentlemen, whose duty it was to introduce the foreign guests to the Imperial couple. Of these four, two were ex-students of Yung Wing's Educational Mission to the United States. They were Liang Tun-yen and Admiral Tsai Ting-kan. It is one of the oddest commentaries on modern China that in this last little episode of the Manchus in the Imperial City we still find two of Yung Wing's "Americans" bridging the gap between the Chinese and the Western worlds. It had been their function for forty years and they remained steadfast to it to the very end.

Shortly after this scene the young emperor and his bride were driven from the Imperial City by one of the many warlords who were ravaging China at this time. In direct violation of the Abdication Agreement of 1912, the emperor's titles and palaces were taken from him and he became simply Citizen Henry Pu Yi. The sole voice raised in protest against this betrayal of the pledged word of the republic was that of Tong Shao-yi. From his home in Tientsin, he had the courage to assert his indignation at the treatment of the last Manchu emperor and to state his belief that according to the Agreement of 1912, the republic had no right to take away the property and titles of the emperor. Furthermore, Tong pointed out that there was nothing in the Agreement to prevent the deposed monarch from returning to Manchuria, there to resume sway over the original homeland of the Manchus. Later, when the Japanese seized Manchuria and placed Henry Pu Yi upon the throne of the puppet state of Manchoukuo, this assertion of Tong Shao-yi was recalled. He was accused of being pro-Japanese at a time when such an accusation was almost tantamount to a death sentence. On September 30, 1938, assassins entered his home in Peking and struck him down. Thus died the most famous of the members of the Educational Mission of 1871. His influence upon the emergence of modern China, and especially his part in 1911 in bringing about the republic, was of greatest importance. Unlike Sun Yat-sen, he came to the making of the republic not as a professional revolutionary but as an experienced and loyal servant of the Manchu dynasty. At the fateful Shanghai peace conference of December 1911, Tong, when once he had grasped the widespread desire for a republic, courageously came out for the abdication of the Manchus. It was this decision of Tong Shao-yi which caused Yüan Shih-k'ai, isolated in Peking, to advise the emperor to abdicate in favor of a republic. In the welter of later politics, the services of Tong Shao-yi at this crucial juncture have either been forgotten or have been overshadowed by the great figure of Sun Yat-sen. The unfortunate circumstances of his death have further tended to obscure his influence upon the formation of the republic. Nevertheless, his influence, coming as it did at such a critical moment, was decisive. No one can deny him his rightful place as one of the founders of the Chinese Republic.

CHAPTER X

EPILOGUE

I shall never forget a little scene that took place in Shanghai in the summer of 1940. It was a simple everyday occurrence, nothing more than a few very old Chinese gentlemen gathered as my guests around a table in the dining room of one of Shanghai's modern hotels. If the other occupants of the room noticed us at all, they might have thought it strange that I should have chosen for my little dinner party only very old men, all of them many years my seniors. Any American who chanced to pass our table and who caught a fragment of our conversation would have been no doubt startled to catch choice bits of American slang intermingled with our exchange of courtesies and to hear these Chinese gentlemen in their long silk gowns address each other by nicknames more familiar to an American schoolyard than to a Shanghai hotel. Such a passing American would have been even more surprised to discover that these nicknames had really been earned over sixty years ago in the schoolyards and playgrounds of a score of New England towns. These old men were some of the very few surviving members of the Chinese Educational Mission. Altogether there are still about a dozen of them living in the port cities of China. Some are comfortably off, occupying spacious homes and surrounded by their numerous grown sons and daughters. To others Fate has not been so kind. Several of them were robbed of the material fruits of long years of loyal service to China when the Japanese invasion of Shanghai in 1931 destroyed their homes.

I particularly recall the brave figure of Captain Yung Leang as he sat at the table, merry and joking about the old days at Hartford. His old friends still called him "By Jinks Johnny". His life had been full of ups and downs and a final stroke of bad fortune had robbed him of his home in Shanghai when a Japanese shell had destroyed it. All Johnny Leang saved from the wreckage was a photograph of his beloved dead wife. Now he lives in modest quarters, which he shares with his young grandchildren, while his sons are off fighting China's battles.

Another of the old men was Chung Mun-yew, the "Munney" of the old Hartford days and the lightest coxswain ever to coach Yale to victory over Harvard. The youngest of the students, today he retains much of the vigor which has always been his. I had the opportunity to visit him in his home in Shanghai. There I met his three beautiful daughters, all of whom had been to school in America. Fortune had always been kind to "Munney," and when he arrived that evening he came in a big Packard with a chauffeur and guard.

Perhaps I did not quite realize at the moment how really kind were these old men in accepting my invitation to dinner. Shanghai in 1940 was no place to be seen in public for men with any pretensions to wealth. The city was overrun with gangsters whose kidnapping and murdering made it dangerous for anyone to venture outside the gates of the compounds in which were their homes.

Sitting and chatting with them, I realized how profoundly their ten years' sojourn in the United States, occurring as it did when they were young and impressionable, had affected their lives. The returned student of today is such a common figure in the life of the port cities that his Western education gives him no particular distinction. But these men, when they returned to China in 1881, were unique in their accomplishments and their experiences. In fact so much so that they remained apart from the swirling currents of Oriental life around them. Their experiences had made them strangers in their own land and to a marked degree they had remained strangers. Always in talking to them and being with them, I felt this apartness. They had served China faithfully and magnificently but more

161

as foreigners employed in the Chinese service than as Chinese. Being with them I recalled Yung Wing's determination to so saturate the students with an American viewpoint that they would be able to overcome the hostile atmosphere which would always surround their efforts to introduce western technology into China. Perhaps Yung Wing realized that this was the only way in which the students would ever be able to resist the inertia of Chinese life.

In Tientsin I spent many hours in the spacious home of Liang Yu-ho, who in the old days had done so much for the promotion of railroads in China. Nearly always one or the other of his two doctor sons would come in from their private hospital attached to the house to join in the conversation. One of them had followed his father to America and spoke English with an amusing Boston intonation. The other had been educated in England and his speech was pure Oxford. Liang Yu-ho, although in his eighty-third year, remained a smiling vigorous man who recalled with relish the experiences of his earlier years. A few months after my visit he died.

In Peking the hand of the invading Japanese lay heavily upon the old Imperial city. Never shall I forget the morning when, after much seeking, I found the residence of Ouyang King. He had served the Chinese Government, both Empire and Republic, in many important diplomatic posts, but on that morning I found him alone and in despair. His five sons had just been arrested by the puppet Chinese authorities in Peking. The Japanese had decided that the younger people of the city were getting restive so they had instigated wholesale arrests of students and young men and women. No charges were brought against most of those arrested, but they were kept in horrible conditions of confinement and then gradually released a few at a time. It was thought that by this means their spirit would be broken. Before I left Peking all five of Ouyang's sons had been released but all of them were left sick in minds and bodies by their ordeal. Shortly afterwards, Ouyang died of shock and worry.

Thus are quickly passing away the few survivors of the Chinese Educational Mission. Meanwhile among the hills of Shensi and on the plains of Szechuan there is arising a new China, a China filled with the spirit of a reinvigorated national life and a new found patriotism. It is the renaissance of a whole people rising to defend their soil against a ruthless invader. The streams that have flowed from the past to make up the torrent of new China have many sources. Surely not the least important is the one that flows from Yung Wing poring over his English lessons in Mrs. Gutzlaff's school in Macao and widening through the years until today it embraces that great army of "returned students" who have done so much to revitalize the ancient civilization of China with the new wine of Occidental technology.

It would be useless to adorn the preceding pages with an imposing bibliography of books, articles from learned journals, and other conventional sources of information. Any books or articles I have used have been largely useful in checking dates and small points of information. For the most part the materials upon which the story of the Chinese Educational Mission to the United States is based are personal in nature, consisting mostly of old letters, notes of conversations, short auto-biographies compiled at my request by the few surviving members of the Mission, or biographies supplied by the sons and daughters of the deceased. As I look back over the search for such precious personal materials as the above, I recall some unfortunate incidents in the search. For instance, in the 1931 bombardment of Shanghai by the Japanese, the correspondence and diary of Yung Wing was lost. What a wealth of material for a study of the emergence of modern China his papers must have contained! Likewise I recall the carelessness of a relative which permitted a lifetime correspondence between a New England lady and several of the former's students who had lived with her family in Hartford when she was a girl to be burned up as rubbish of no value to anyone. But against these more unfortunate incidents I must place the good fortune which almost at the outset of my interest in the Yung Wing boys and their careers brought me into contact with Mr. Arthur G. Robinson, who has charge of the Walker Missionary Home at Auburndale, Massachusetts. A chance mention to a friend about Yung Wing and the band of young Chinese lads he brought to the United States in 1872 brought the advice to write to an A. G. Robinson whom my informant thought was still living in Tientsin where he had been an educational missionary for many years. Months after the dispatch of a letter to Tientsin there came a warm invitation from Mr. Robinson to visit him in Auburndale where he had recently moved and which was only a few hours away from where I was then living. A short visit with Mr. Robinson resulted in his most generously making available to me the materials on the Educational Mission which he had collected during his years in China. Much of it was derived from his personal friendship with the members of the Mission and only could have been collected in the constant association of friendship and neighborliness with them. These materials together with a large collection of photographs are now deposited in the Library of the State College of Washington.

Again I recall the kindness and interest of Captain Yung Leang in Shanghai and Mr. Y. T. Woo in Tientsin, who despite their advanced years and the troublous conditions around them were ever faithful in their efforts to collect from their old comrades of the Hartford days letters, photographs, and other materials bearing upon their careers. To Captain Yung Leang I particularly owe a debt of gratitude for his careful compilation of the names of the one hundred and twenty students who came to America with the Educational Mission.

As to the background materials, the series of monographs by Professor Gideon Chen of Yenching University on such early reformers as Lin Tse-hsü, Tsêng Kuo-fan, and Tso Tsung-t'ang are invaluable for the study of the influence of the Occident upon modern China. No satisfactory studies of Li Hung-chang or Yüan Shih-k'ai exist. Their careers must be pieced together from many sources. Yung Wing's story, *My Life in China and America,* although it must be used with caution, is obviously indispensible. The materials in Chinese are scattered largely throughout the collections of the official papers of Tsêng Kuo-fan and Li Hung-chang. There are a few references to the Mission in the Records of the Ch'ing Dynasty, the *Ta Ch'ing li ch'ao shih lu.* These references to the Mission in Chinese official documents I have brought together in an article, "The Chinese Educational Mission to the United States, 1871-1888" which appeared in the November, 1941, issue of the *Far Eastern Quarterly*. Outside of these official sources, Chinese writers who have concerned themselves with the Mission have done little more than summarize the story as told by Yung Wing.

I can almost recall the exact moment of the origin of my interest in the Chinese Educational Mission and in the subsequent careers of the students when they returned to China. My wife and I were driving from the Pacific Coast to take up a two year residence in New England. We knew not what lay ahead as neither of us had been to the eastern United States. One day as we were speeding along the endless U. S. No. 30, somewhere in the vicinity of Cheyenne, Wyoming, we began to speculate upon our future activities in New England, and I suggested that in order to give direction to the week-end trips we were planning that we should try to find out when the first Chinese appeared in the United States. Once in New Haven we soon began to hear about Yung Wing and the boys of the Educational Mission. When we discovered that Yung Wing had arrived at Monson Academy in Monson, Massachusetts, in 1847, we felt that we were near the earliest Chinese, but soon afterwards we discovered that as early as 1817 a Chinese was receiving some education in the Foreign Mission School in the little village of Cornwall, Connecticut. It subsequently turned out that at least five Chinese attended this school. A perusal of early New England newspapers led us to the humorous incident of John Jacob Astor's Chinese mandarin. This was the incident in which Astor, in order to get a ship out to Canton through the embargo of 1808, "discovered" on the New York waterfront a respectable Chinese merchant from Canton who was exceedingly desirous of returning home and who threatened dire consequences to the commerce of the United States at that port unless he were enabled speedily to return thither. Astor's competitors vowed that the Chinese merchant was none other than a chance Chinese sailor who had become stranded in New York; nevertheless on the plea of maintaining amicable relations between the United States and China, Astor was given a permit to take the ship "Beaver" out through the embargo with his mandarin as passenger.

We now thought that surely we had found the first Chinese to visit the United States, but a reading through Burnett's *Letters of the Continental Congress* led to an investigation of five Chinese who in 1785 had become wards of the Continental Congress until a way could be found to ship them back to their homes from whence they had been "shanghaied" by a rascally ship captain. They had been brought to the United States on the ship "Pallas" which dropped anchor off the city of Baltimore in August, 1785. The petition to the Continental Congress, with the signatures of the five Chinese attached, in which they supplicated for their return home is still preserved in the Library of Congress in Washington.

Beyond this our research has not carried us, but I surmise that with sufficient diligence a Chinese could be found serving in Washington's army during the Revolutionary War. I once carelessly bet that I could find the record of a Chinese who fought in the Civil War. That proved simple for a little research soon led to the paper of Dr. William F. Worner, read before the Lancaster Historical Society of Pennsylvania, on "A Chinese Soldier in the Civil War" in which he relates the experiences of Hong Neok Woo, who served in the Pennsylvania Militia.

These earlier Chinese, however, were strays who added little to the cultural interchange between the world's oldest and newest empires. With Yung Wing and his boys it was different. They definitely are the starting place for any study on the Chinese side of Sino-American cultural relations. The above pages present no definitive study. The meagerness of the sources made such an aim impossible. I have exhausted every source I could find. The "boys" of the Mission were not prone to keep diaries or carefully file away their correspondence. Their activities will have to be fitted into the larger picture of the transformation of old China into the emerging China of today. It is with this hope that I have attempted to record the achievements and influence upon Modern China of this small but potent group of China's first band of "returned students".

T. E. La Fargue

Pullman, Washington
    June 30, 1942.

Boxer Rebellion: a series of anti-foreign movements which broke out in 1900. The name was derived from a secret society whose members called themselves "The Public-Spirited Harmonious Boxers." Their aim was to drive out the foreigners.

Chang Chih-tung, 1835-1909: Founder of the great Han Yeh P'ing iron works at Hanyang and author of "Exhortation to Learn," a famous plea for reform.

Ch'en Lan-pin: The Co-Commissioner, with Yung Wing, of the Chinese Educational Mission to the United States. In 1878 he became China's first Minister to the United States.

China Merchants Steam Navigation Company: A company founded in 1874 under the sponsorship of Li Hung-chang. The object of the founders was to compete with the foreign steamship lines for the coastal and river commerce.

Chow Wan: One of the six pupils of the first class of the Morrison Educational Society school opened at Canton in 1836.

Examination system, Metropolitan examinations: The system whereby through an ascending series of prefectual, provincial, and metropolitan examinations, based largely on the Confucian classics, government officials were chosen.

Hsüan T'ang: Reign title of the last Manchu Emperor. He was a child at the time of the Revolution of 1911. At present he is the Emperor of Manchoukuo.

Hundred Days' Reforms: A series of edicts issued by the Emperor Kuang Hsü in the summer of 1898. The edicts were countermanded by order of the Empress Dowager, Tz'u Hsi, and the Emperor was thrown into prison.

Kiangnan Arsenal: Founded by Tsêng Kuo-fan at Shanghai. Attached to it was a translation Bureau which translated over two hundred scientific works into Chinese.

Kuang Hsü: Reign title of the emperor who ruled from 1889 to 1908. He was the nephew of the Empress Dowager, Tz'u Hsi. She dominated affairs during most of his reign. See Hundred Days' Reforms.

Li Hung-chang, 1822-1901: famous Viceroy of the Metropolitan province of Chihli. He was joint sponsor with Tsêng Kuo-fan of the Chinese Educational Mission.

Li Kan: One of the six pupils of the first class of the Morrison Educational Society School opened in Canton in 1836.

Lin Tse-hsü: The Commissioner sent in 1839 to Canton to suppress the opium traffic. His seizure of the opium held by foreigners brought on the Opium War of 1840-1842.

Memorials to the Throne: In Imperial China new legislation was proposed to the Throne in a memorial presented by some prominent official. If the proposal was accepted, a decree was issued embodying the new law.

Morrison, Robert, 1782-1834: The first Protestant missionary to China. He arrived in Canton in 1807 and died there in 1834.

Northern Squadron, or Pei Hai Yang Chun: The fleet of naval vessels organized by Li Hung-chang and attached to the Viceroy of Chihli.

Opium Wars of 1840 *and* 1856: The war of 1840 between Great Britain and China which arose out of the Chinese Government's attempt to suppress the opium traffic is usually referred to as the "Opium War." The war between China and Great Britain and France which lasted from 1856 to 1860 is usually known as the "Arrow War."

Sino-French War, 1882-1885. The war between France and China in which France successfully challenged China's claim to suzerainty over Tonking.

Sino-Japanese War, 1894-1895. This war arose out of the contest between China and Japan for the control of Korea.

The Southern Squadron; Nan Hai Yang Chun: The fleet attached to the Viceroyalty of Kiangsi, Anhwei, and Kiangsu. The headquarters of this viceroyalty were at Nanking.

Taotai: The Intendant of a Circuit of which there were ninety-five in China. He had supervision of several prefectures or counties.

T'ai P'ing Rebellion: This rebellion ravaged China from 1850 to 1864. Its object was to overthrow the Manchu dynasty and to establish the T'ai P'ing or Great Peace Dynasty.

Tong King-sing: A fellow student of Yung Wing in the Morrison Educational Society School opened in Canton in 1836. He later founded the China Merchants Steam Navigation Company. He also developed the K'aiping mines and built China's first railway.

Tsêng Kuo-fan: The great reformer who with Li Hung-chang sponsored the Chinese Educational Mission.

Tsing Hua College: Established in 1911 in order to prepare and select students to be sent to the United States under the terms of the agreement whereby the United States returned a portion of the Boxer Idemnity to China.

Tso Tsung-t'ang, 1812-1885: Founder of the Foochow Arsenal and Naval College.

Tz'u Hsi, 1835-1908: The Empress Dowager. The reign name of the Manchu princess, Yehonala, and widow of the Emperor Hsien Feng. She dominated the Chinese Court from 1875 to 1908.

Viceroy: A Governor-General of one or more provinces. Within his viceroyalty he was supreme in control of all civil and military affairs, including relations with foreigners. He could be recalled or transferred by the Throne.

Wong Foon: One of six students of the first class of the Morrison Educational Society School opened in Canton in 1836.

He later studied medicine at the University of Edinburgh and returned to China to become China's first Western-trained physician.

Wong Hsing: One of the six pupils of the first class of the Morrison Educational Society School opened in Canton in 1836. He was also a teacher in the Chinese Educational Mission.

Woo Tzê-têng: Commissioner of the Chinese Educational Mission to the United States from 1878 to 1881. It was his unfavorable reports that were largely responsible for the recall of the Mission.

Yüan Shih-k'ai, 1860-1916: Chinese Resident in Korea from 1884-1904. Later Acting Viceroy of Chihli and President of the Republic.

A List of the Students of the Chinese Educational Mission*

First Detachment (arrived in the United States in 1872)

Name	Age upon arrival in the U. S.	Subsequent Occupation
1. Tsai Shou Kee	13	Director of Customs
2. Chung Mun Yew	13	Railroad Director
3. Woo Yang Tsang	12	Mining Engineer
4. Low Kwok Sui	12	Mining Engineer
5. Ouyang King	14	Diplomatic Service
6. Young Shang Him	10	Naval Officer
7. Wong Chung Liang	15	Railway Director
8. Kwong Young Kong	10	Mining Engineer
9. Tsai Cum Shang	14	Railway Director
10. Chang Hon Yen	13	Lawyer in Honolulu and San Francisco
11. Liang Tun Yen	15	Cabinet Officer and Minister of Foreign Affairs
12 New Shan Chow	11	Telegraph Service
13. Paun Min Chung	10	Died in the United States
14. Liu Chia Chew	12	No known occupation
15. Jeme Tien Yau	12	Railroad Engineer—Builder of the Peking-Kalgan Railway
16. Wong Sic Pao	13	Career unknown — probably died at an early age.
17. Wong Kai Kah	13	Diplomatic Service
18. Ho Ting Liang	13	Naval Doctor
19. Chun Kee Young	13	Died at an early age
20. Tso Ki Foo	13	Private business in Shanghai
21. Tan Yew Fun	13	Died in the United States
22. Ching Ta Hee	14	Teacher of Engineering
23. Luk Wing Chuan	14	Consular Service
24. Shih Kin Tong	14	Died at an early age
25. Ting Sze Chung	14	Naval Officer
26. Chun Wing Kwai	14	Mining Engineer
27. Chung Ching Shing	14	Interpreter in the United States Consular Service
28. Chin Mon Fay	14	Consular Service
29. Sze Kin Yung	15	Private business in China
30. Tseng Tuh Kun	16	Newspaper Editor and subordinate government official

Second Detachment (arrived in the United States in 1873)

Name	Age upon arrival in the U. S.	Subsequent Occupation
31. Tsai Ting Kan	13	Admiral in the Navy
32. Woo Ying Fo	14	Admiral in the Navy

*Most of the names are given in their original Cantonese form.

Name	Age upon arrival in the U. S.	Subsequent Occupation
33. Woo Chung Yen	14	Consular Service
34. Yung Kwai	14	Diplomatic Service
35. Sue Yi Chew	14	Diplomatic Service
36. Won Bing Chung	21	Chinese Maritime Customs
37. Ting Sung Kih	14	Chinese Maritime Customs
38. Lok Sik Kwai	13	Railroad & Mining Engineer
39. Liang Kin Wing	14	Chinese Telegraph Service
40. Lee Yen Fu (Yen Fu-lee)	13	Newspaper Reporter in the United States
41. Wong Yau Chang	13	Teacher
42. Fong Pah Liang	13	Telegraph Service
43. Chang Hsiang Woo	11	Diplomatic Service
44. Chun Kin Sing	14	Career unknown
45. Wong Fung Kai	14	Diplomatic Service
46. Tseng Poo	unknown	Mining Engineering
47. Yung Shang Kun	unknown	Teacher
48. Lee Kwai Pan	14	Tea business in New York
49. Tong Kwo On (Tong Kai-son)	14	Mining Engineer
50. Sung Mon Wai	13	Naval Officer
51. Chang Yau Kung	12	Died at an early age
52. Ting Kwai Ting	13	Died at an early age
53. Tong Yuen Chan	13	Telegraph Service
54. Chun Pay Hu	11	Interpreter in the United States Consular Service
55. Kwong King Huan	13	Died at an early age
56. Kwong Wing Chung	13	Naval Officer
57. Liang Pao Shi	11	Railway Official
58. Liang Pao Chew	13	Mining Engineer
59. Chuck Yen Chi	12	Died at an early age
60. Wong Liang Ting	13	Railway Official and Consular Service

Third Detachment (arrived in the United States in 1874)

Name	Age	Subsequent Occupation
61. Tong Shao Yi	12	Cabinet Officer and Envoy
62. Liang Yu Ho (M. T. Liang)	12	Railway Official
63. Chow Chang Ling (Sir Shouson Chow)	14	Railway Official and Business Man
64. Kwong King Yang	12	Railway Engineer
65. Chu Pao Fay	12	Telegraph Service
66. Young Yew Huan	10	Business Man

Name	Age upon arrival in the U. S.	Subsequent Occupation
67. Tsao Ka-hsiang	11	Naval Officer
68. Woo King Yung	11	Naval Officer
69. Chow Wan Pung	11	Telegraph Service
70. Loo Ssu Wha	11	Mining Engineer and Railway Official
71. Lin Pay Chuan	12	Railway Official
72. Chu Chun Pan	11	Naval Officer
73. Tong Chi Yao	13	Railway Official
74. Ching Ta Yeh	12	Telegraph Service
75. Sit Yau Fu	13	Naval Officer
76. Chu Chi Shuan	12	Died at an early age
77. Tsao Ka Chuck	12	Died in the United States
78. Tsao Mao Hsang	10	Naval Doctor
79. Chu Sik Shao	10	Telegraph Service
80. Won Wai Shing	10	Business Man
81. Yuen Chan Kwon	12	Telegraph Service
82. Kee Tsu Yi	12	Government Official
83. Kong Kin Ling	12	Died when young
84. Kwong Yen Chow	12	Mining Engineer
85. Yang Sew Nan	13	Naval Officer
86. Wong Kwei Liang	13	Naval Officer
87. Yang Chan Ling	12	Railway Official
88. Jang Ting Shan	13	Engineer
89. Sun Kwong Ming	14	Telegraph Service
90. Shen Ke Shu	13	Railway Official

Fourth Detachment (arrived in the United States in 1875)

Name	Age	Subsequent Occupation
91. Liu Yu Lin	13	Consular Service
92. Kwong Kwok Kong	13	Naval Officer
93. Kwong Pin Kong	13	Naval Officer
94. Wong Yew Chong	13	Railway Official and Business Man
95. Woo Huan Yung	13	Telegraph Service
96. Chow Chuen Kan	13	Railway and Mining Engineer
97. Paun Sze Chi	11	Government Official
98. Lok Teh Chang	13	Telegraph Service
99. Tao Ting King	12	Telegraph Service
100. Woo Kee Tsao	12	Naval Officer
101. Lin Yuen Shing	14	Telegraph Service
102. Tan Yew Fong	10	Died at an early age
103. Shen Mou Yang	12	Telegraph Service
104. Chun Shao Chang	13	Died at an early age
105. Tong Wing Ho	13	Government Official
106. Tong Wing Chun	14	Business man

Name	Age upon arrival in the U.S.	Subsequent Occupation
107. Liang Ao Ting	11	Career unknown
108. Chen Fu Tseng	14	Died at an early age
109. Lin Yuen Fai	15	Doctor
110. Chin Kin Kwai	12	Naval Officer
111. Kin Ta Ting	13	Doctor
112. Shen Teh Yew	14	Businessman
113. Shen Teh Fai	12	Died at an early age
114. Shen Shao Chang	11	Naval Officer
115. Lee Yu Kin	11	Doctor
116. Wong Yen Bin	12	Died at an early age
117. Fung Bing Chung	12	Telegraph Service
118. Liang Pe Yuk	12	
(Sir Chun Tung Liang Shing)		Diplomatic Service
119. Chow Chuen Ao	13	Died at an early age
120. Wong Chu Lin	13	Naval Officer

INDEX

and concessions, 121
and Franco-Chinese troops, 6
and naval service, 70
and Opium Wars, 3, 170
and railways, 105, 127-128
and Sino-French War, 8, 72-73, 170
and War of 1856-1860, 13
and Yüan Shih-k'ai, 155
Fryer, Dr. John, 27

G

German interests
and Banking Consortium, 152
and Chang Chih-tung, 127-128
and concessions, 121-122
and expulsion of German citizens, 137
and Kiaochow base, 153
and Liang Tun-yen, 130-131
and military instructors, 9-10
and Yung Wing, 64
Giquel, Prosper, 6, 70
Gordon, General Charles "Chinese," 3, 25
Grant, President, 49, 50
Great Northern Telegraph Company, 85-88, 133
Greenfield, Mass., 81
Gutzlaff, Mrs., 18-19
Gutzlaff, Rev. Charles, 18

H

Hai Kuo t'u Chih (Description of the Maritime Nations, Wei Yuan), 20, 67
Han Yeh P'ing Iron and Steel Works, Hanyang/Hankow, 9, 123
Hankow
and industry, 9, 123, 125
and Liang Tun-yen, 125
and railways, 127, 128
and revolution, 146, 148, 149
and Yung Sing-kew, 143
Hankow-Szechuan railway line, 128
Hanyang, 9, 146, 149
Harriman, E. H., 122
Hart, Sir Robert, 62
Hartford, Conn.
and Bartlett family, 20, 35, 124
and Chinese students, 34-35, 37, 53
and Educational Mission headquarters, 40-41
and Liang Tun-yen, 124
and Woo Tzê-têng, 44
and Yung Kwai, 45
and Yung Wing, 43, 61
Hartford High School, Conn., 108, 118, 124, 133
Hartford Primary School, Conn., 133
Harvard College, 45
Henry Pu Yi (earlier Emperor Hsüan T'ung), 80, 150, 156-159, 169
Hobson, Dr. Benjamin, 19, 69
Hong Kong

and financial loans, 127
and Sir Shouson Chow, 116, 136
and telegraph lines, 85, 86
and Wong Kai-kah, 58
and Yung Sing-kew, 143
and Yung Wing, 64
Hong Neok Woo, 167
Hoover, Herbert C., 98
Hoy Yung (Yung Sing-kew), 143-144
Hsu Shon, 69
Hsüan T'ung, Emperor, 80, 150, 156-159, 169
Hu Wei-teh, 148
Hui-Ch'eng arsenal, 5
Hukuang railway concession, 126-130
Hundred Days' Reforms (1898), 11, 169
Hyde, Deacon Alexander, 39

I

Ichang, 135
Imperial Chinese Customs, 116
Imperial family, 150, 156-158
see also Emperors, Empress Dowager, Princes
Imperial Maritime Customs, 125
Imperial Northern Government Telegraph College, 89
Imperial Railway Administration, 113, 114, 126
Imperial Telegraph Administration, 89, 91, 92
International Consortium loan (1911), 131, 151-152
iron foundries, 9, 123, 125

J

Jang Ting-seong, 142
Jann coupling, 142
Japanese interests
and Banking Consortium, 152
and concessions, 121
and Korea, 11, 116-118
and Liaotung Peninsula, 133
and Manchuria, 119-123, 131-132, 136, 154, 158
and naval supplies, 10
and railways, 112
and Twenty-one Demands, 154
and World War I, 153-155
see also Sino-Japanese War
Jehol silver mines, 97
Jeme Tien-yau (Jeme Tien-yow), 60, 108, 110, 111-113
Jenchuan, 136
Jerome, Elizabeth Maud, 142
Jerome, Gilbert, 142
Johnstone, Mr., 157

179

and Liang Yu-ho, 116, 135
resistance to, 2
and Sir Shouson Chow, 135
and Yung Wing, 63-64
Records of the Ch'ing Dynasty, 165
Reinsch, Paul, 152-153
Rensselaer Polytechnic Institute, N.Y., 81
Repatriation Bureau (Bureau for the Repatria-
tion of Enemies), 137
Republic of China established, 145-159
Revolution of 1911, 130, 136, 145-159
Reynolds, Mr., 85
Robinson, Arthur G., 164-165
Rockhill, W. W., 125
Roosevelt, President Theodore, 122, 123
Root, Elihu, 122
Root-Takahira accord (1908), 122-123
Royal School of Mines, London, 97
Russian interests
and Banking Consortium, 152
and Chinese monarchy, 155
and concessions, 121
and K'aiping mines, 98
in Korea, 118
in Manchuria, 120, 122, 131
in railways, 112-113
Russo-Japanese War (1905), 91, 110, 112, 134

S

Sah Chen-ping, Admiral, 148
St. Louis Exposition, 91
St. Petersburg, 139
San Francisco, 37, 53, 141
Scotland, 21
Seoul, 117, 118
Sequestration of Enemy Property, 137
Seward, F. S., 1
Shanghai
and Chung Mun-yew, 113
and Educational Mission Bureau, 33
and Educational Mission students, 34,
36-37, 54, 58-59, 160-161
and foreigners, 36
Kiangnan Arsenal, 26-27, 29, 68-70, 81, 169
and M. T. Liang, 110-111
and peace conference (1911), 148-150, 159
and railways, 100-102, 113-114
and telegraph services, 83, 85-86, 92
and Tong Shao-yi, 147-151, 159
and Tsai Shou-kee, 133
and Tsai Ting-kan, 80
and Tso Tsung-t'ang, 6
and Yung Leang, 165
and Yung Wing, 28, 63-64, 164
Shanghai Customs Intendant, 113
Shanghai-Nanking railway, 113, 114
Shanghai peace conference (1911), 149-150, 159
Shanhaikuan, 104

Shantung, 153
Sheffield Scientific School, Yale College, 141
Shen Ke-shu, 114
Shen Kung-pao, 91, 129
Shen Shao-chang, 75
Sheperd, E. T., 95
Shing Sun-wei, 63
Shortrede, Andrew, 21
silver mining, 97
Sino-American Treaty (1868, Burlingame
Treaty), 32-33, 41, 46-48, 139
Sino-British Wars (Opium Wars), 3, 5, 13, 20,
67, 170
Sino-French War (1882-1885), 8, 72-73, 170
Sino-Japanese War (1894-1895), 170
and Chang Chih-tung, 10
and Educational Mission students, 75-78
and Li Hung-chang, 5, 71, 72-73, 104
and Tsai Ting-kan, 79
and Yüan Shih-k'ai, 11, 117
Sit Yan-fu, 74
Smith, Annie, 39
Soochow arsenal, 68
source materials, 164-168
South Africa, 140
Southern Seas Squadron (Nan Yang Hai Chun),
70, 171
Springfield, Mass., 46, 78, 108
Springfield High School, Mass., 45, 108
State College of Washington, 165
Steel making, 9, 123, 125
Stevens School of Technology, Hartford, 108
Straight, Willard, 119-123, 129
Straits Settlement, 140
Sun Yat-sen, 143, 145, 150-151, 153, 159
Swatow, 58
Szechuan, 129, 130

T

*Ta Ch'ing Li Ch'ao Shih Lu (Records of the
Ch'ing Dynasty),* 165
T'ai P'ing Rebellion (1850-1864), 3-4, 5-7,
23-25, 68, 171
Taku, 60, 72, 79, 83, 94
Taku Bar, 103
Tan Yew-fun, 46
Tao Ting-king, 92
Telegraph Administration, 89, 91, 92
telegraph network, 2, 5, 83-92, 133
telegraph schools/colleges, 58-60, 89-90, 92,
124, 140
Tibet, 119, 132
Tientsin
and A. G. Robinson, 164
arsenal (West Arsenal), 108
and coal supplies, 94, 95, 98
and Liang Tun-yen, 125

183

184